ROBERT GARDNER'S CHALLENGING SCIENCE EXPERIMENTS

Other Books by Robert Gardner

Experimenting with Energy Conservation

Experimenting with Illusions

Experimenting with Inventions

Experimenting with Light

Experimenting with Sound

Ideas for Science Projects

More Ideas for Science Projects

Robert Gardner's Favorite Science Experiments

ROBERT GARDNER'S CHALLENGING SCIENCE EXPERIMENTS

by ROBERT GARDNER

FRANKLIN WATTS
NEW YORK / CHICAGO / LONDON / TORONTO / SYDNEY

Photographs copyright ©: Education Development Center: pp. 35, 37, 52; Robert Gardner: p. 45; The Harold E. Edgerton 1992 Trust: p. 74; Stock Boston: pp. 95 (Lionel Delevingne), 164 top (Frank Siteman), Photo Researchers, Inc./National Audubon Society/John Hendry Jr.: p. 105; Susan Van Etten: pp. 119, 164 bottom, Randy Matusow: pp. 124, 148.

Library of Congress Cataloging-in-Publication Data

Gardner, Robert, 1929–
[Challenging science experiments]
Robert Gardner's challenging science experiments /
by Robert Gardner.
p. cm.
Includes bibliographical references and index.
Summary: Presents easy-to-prepare scientific experiments that demonstrate principles of physics, chemistry, astronomy, and biology.
ISBN 0-531-11090-7 (lib. bdg.) — ISBN 0-531-15671-0 (pbk.)
1. Science—Experiments—Juvenile literature.   [1. Science—Experiments.   2. Experiments.]   I. Title.   II. Title:
Challenging science experiments.
Q164.G315   1993
507.8—dc20   92-21116 CIP AC

CONTENTS

TO THE READER

I was delighted when Franklin Watts asked me to write a book of challenging experiments. Few authors and teachers can review and cull what they have done over many years, so I regard the opportunity to write this book as one of the privileges of having lived and worked for a long time. I hope you will enjoy the experiments found here as much as I enjoyed preparing them and writing about them.

Some of the experiments have appeared in other books I've written in a somewhat different format. Others—experiments that I used with my own students during my many years of teaching science—have never been published before. None of the experiments is very difficult to do, but I hope you'll find that the analysis of the results of at least some of them will challenge you. You'll find some more challenging than others, and something that is challenging to you may seem quite straightforward to a friend and vice versa. That's why you may find it fruitful to work with a friend or a small group of friends.

To make things easier, I have included a list of the things you'll need for each experiment. You can find most of these materials in your home or school. Anything else you may need shouldn't be very expensive. You'll probably be able to find it in a hardware or electronics store, or at one of the science supply houses listed in the Appendix.

In the introductions to some of the experiments, I've explained what I like about them or what is special or challenging about them, and I may tell you what *I* hope you'll learn from it. It may not be the same reason *you* like the experiment. Of course, the choice is yours; you're the reader. You can choose those experiments that you think you'll enjoy doing most. If you don't like the experiment, you don't have to do it. But at least read why I've included it. Maybe then you'll see it's worth doing even if at first you don't think you'll enjoy it.

Some of the tools and procedures used in science can be dangerous if you are careless or haven't been trained to use a particular piece of equipment. **I've tried to alert you to any potential danger or procedure that requires caution by using bold type.** In a few places, for reasons of safety, I've indicated that you should ask an adult to help you. In anything that you do, keep in mind the following rules about safety.

SAFETY RULES

1. Read all instructions carefully before proceeding with an experiment.
2. Maintain a serious attitude while experimenting. Fooling around can be dangerous to you and to others.
3. Wear safety goggles when you are experimenting or are in a laboratory setting. Wear a lab apron if you are working with chemicals.

4. Do not eat or drink while experimenting and do not taste dry chemicals or solutions.

5. Keep flammable materials away from sources of heat.

6. Have safety equipment such as fire extinguishers, fire blankets, and first aid kits nearby while you are experimenting and know where this equipment is.

7. Don't touch glass that has recently been heated; it looks the same as cool glass. Bathe skin burns in cold water or apply ice.

8. Do not touch any high-voltage source or anything connected to a high-voltage source.

9. Never experiment with household electricity without the supervision of a knowledgeable adult.

1

CHALLENGING EXPERIMENTS WITH LIGHT AND ASTRONOMY

I've always been fascinated by light. Not only because it brings vast amounts of information to our eyes as we read or observe the natural world, but because of its properties. When white light is refracted (bent) as it passes from one medium to another, or scattered by the particles in air, its separation into colors provides us with the natural beauty of the sky, sunsets, halos, and rainbows in colors that artists strive to capture on canvas. Reflected light allows us to see our own images in mirrors, gather information about the stars, or view brilliant autumn colors on trees or from the surface of a smooth lake or pond after a second reflection.

Experimenting with light provides many surprises and unexpected pleasures. Once you understand its properties and behavior, you can more fully appreciate the many natural phenomena that you may observe in nature—mirages, twinkling stars, looming, halos, colored rings around the sun and moon, the green flash, moonbows and dew bows, as well as rainbows and sunsets.

MYSTERY IMAGE:
A FUN EXPERIMENT

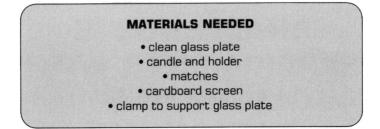

In a dark room, stand a large, clean glass plate about 15 cm (6 in) behind a short burning candle. Then center a large beaker of water the same distance behind the glass plate (about 30 cm from the burning candle).

When you look into the glass, you see a candle burning under water. Of course, what you see in the water is the image of the burning candle. But if the candle is hidden behind a screen, you may be able to convince some naive person that there really is a candle burning under water. What does this suggest about the location of the image of an object placed in front of a smooth, flat reflecting surface?

If you move the candle so it is 25 cm (10 in) in front of the glass plate, where will you have to put the beaker to make the candle's image appear to be under water? If you place the candle 10 cm (4 in) in front of the glass plate, where must you put the beaker to have an underwater image? What does this tell you about the relative positions of object, image, and reflecting surface?

CAN YOU BEND A LIGHT BEAM
WITH A MAGNET?

MATERIALS NEEDED

• laser or
• slide projector, 2 in × 2 in slide, black film, and paper punch
• strong bar or horseshoe magnet
• white screen (paper or cardboard and tape)

After seeing the force exerted on a beam of electrons by a magnetic field perpendicular to their motion, many students have asked me, "Can you bend a light beam with a magnetic field?" My response to them was always "Why don't you try it?"

When I was a young teacher, students would use a slide projector to produce a beam of light. By making a small hole in a piece of black film with a paper punch and mounting the film in an ordinary 2 in × 2 in cardboard slide, they could produce a light beam and focus it on a distant white screen. More recently, students used a laser to produce a narrow beam of light. They seemed to enjoy using the laser; and as long **as they didn't look into its beam, which could be dangerous**, I was happy to have them use it. On the other hand, if you use a laser, you're probably stuck with a red beam. With the slide projector, you can change the color of the beam by placing different colored filters in the slide.

Once a beam could be seen clearly on a distant screen, they would move the pole of a bar magnet close to the beam near the projector or laser. By placing the magnet near the beam's source, any displacement of the beam would be magnified at the position of the screen. Another approach was to place a strong horseshoe magnet near the projector and let the light beam pass between its poles so that the beam was perpendicular to the magnetic field. Then the magnet could be turned 90 degrees so that the beam's path was above the poles and parallel to the field. In this way, they could see the effect of a magnetic field perpendicular to or parallel to the beam.

What do you find when you do this experiment? Does a magnetic field exert a force on a light beam?

MIRRORS IN GLASS AND WATER

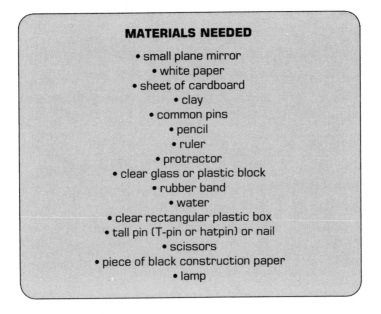

MATERIALS NEEDED

- small plane mirror
- white paper
- sheet of cardboard
- clay
- common pins
- pencil
- ruler
- protractor
- clear glass or plastic block
- rubber band
- water
- clear rectangular plastic box
- tall pin (T-pin or hatpin) or nail
- scissors
- piece of black construction paper
- lamp

You probably know the *law of reflection* for a ray of light reflected from a plane mirror in air—the angles of incidence and reflection are equal. But suppose the reflection takes place in water or in glass. Will the results be the same?

I've always liked this experiment, which is designed to find out what happens when light is reflected in water or glass. The results will probably surprise you and force you to come up with a model that explains the results.

Begin with a small plane mirror in air to confirm the law of reflection. Place the mirror on a piece of white paper resting on a sheet of cardboard. If needed, a small lump of clay can be used to keep the mirror upright. Use a pencil to draw a line along the rear edge of the mirror if it is silvered on the back, or along the front if it is a front surface mirror. After drawing the line, the mirror can be returned to its original position if it should be moved accidentally.

Place two pins—we'll call them the object pins—in a line at some angle to the mirror as shown in Figure 1. Line up two other pins with the *images* of the object pins as seen in the mirror. Use a ruler to draw the two straight lines (rays) made by the pins. Where do they meet? Why do they meet there?

Now remove the mirror and use a protractor to draw a line perpendicular to the line marking the mirror's reflecting surface at the point where the rays meet. How does the angle of incidence ($\angle i$) compare with the angle of reflection ($\angle r$)?

You're ready now for the main part of the experiment. If possible, examine reflection in both glass (or plastic) and water. Fasten the small mirror to a clear glass or plastic block with a rubber band, as shown in Figure 2a, and repeat the experiment. Arrange the pins and mirrors so

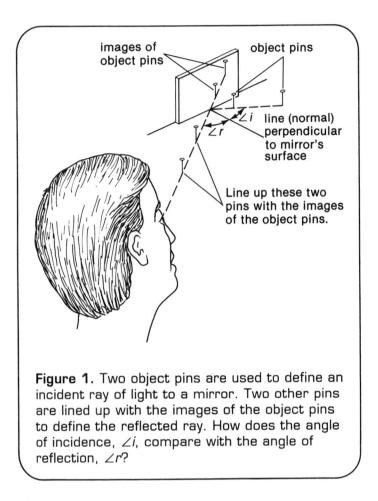

Figure 1. Two object pins are used to define an incident ray of light to a mirror. Two other pins are lined up with the images of the object pins to define the reflected ray. How does the angle of incidence, $\angle i$, compare with the angle of reflection, $\angle r$?

that light from the two object pins must pass through the glass or plastic before being reflected by the mirror. (One pin should be quite close to the block.) After you've lined up two more pins with the images of the object pins, remove the block and draw the two rays. Where do these two rays meet?

Repeat the experiment, but this time place the mirror in a clear water-filled rectangular plas-

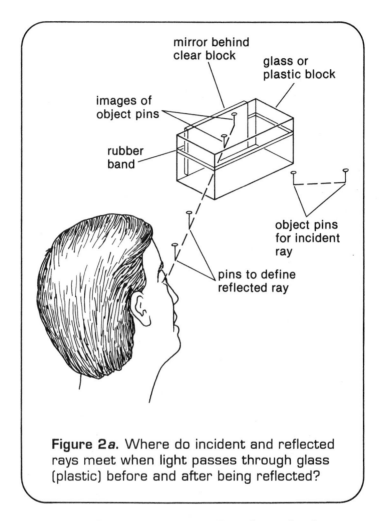

mirror behind
clear block

glass or
plastic block

images of
object pins

rubber
band

object pins
for incident
ray

pins to define
reflected ray

Figure 2a. Where do incident and reflected rays meet when light passes through glass (plastic) before and after being reflected?

tic box as shown in Figure 2b. Where do the rays meet this time?

As a hint, to help you understand what's happening, place a tall pin or a nail behind the clear block or the container of water. The pin should be tall enough to project above the block or water. Look straight through the glass or water so that the top and bottom of the pin are lined up. Slowly

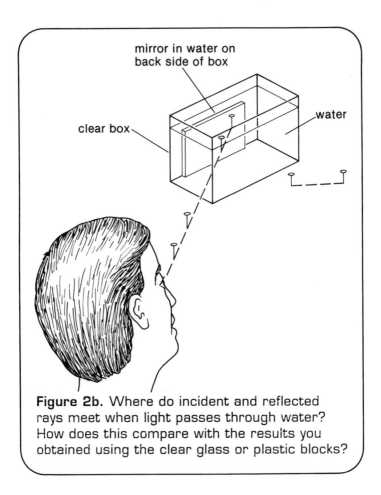

Figure 2b. Where do incident and reflected rays meet when light passes through water? How does this compare with the results you obtained using the clear glass or plastic blocks?

turn the block or box without moving your head. What seems to happen to the top and bottom of the pin?

Devise a model to explain why the incident and reflected rays appear to meet in front of the mirror when the light is reflected in water or glass. Then design an experiment to test your model. If you'd like to have a more visible ray of light for your experiment, use scissors to cut a narrow slit in a piece of black construction paper. By folding the paper, you can make it stand upright on a table or floor. If light from a distant lamp in an otherwise dark room falls on the slit, you will have a thin beam of light on which you can place a glass block or a box of water.

THE INDEX OF REFRACTION

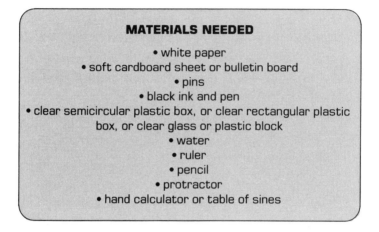

MATERIALS NEEDED

- white paper
- soft cardboard sheet or bulletin board
- pins
- black ink and pen
- clear semicircular plastic box, or clear rectangular plastic box, or clear glass or plastic block
- water
- ruler
- pencil
- protractor
- hand calculator or table of sines

Once my students saw a beam of light reflect from a mirror and measured the angles i and r for different values of i with a protractor (Figure 3), they had no trouble discovering the law of reflection for themselves. They quickly realized that for any angle of incidence, i, the angle of reflection, r, has the same value. Having established the law of reflection, they could understand why the distance D_i from a mirror to the image (behind the mirror) of an object equaled the distance D_o from the mirror to the object (in front of the mirror). See Figure 4.

The law of refraction, however, which estab-

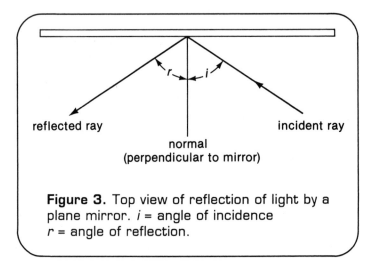

Figure 3. Top view of reflection of light by a plane mirror. i = angle of incidence r = angle of reflection.

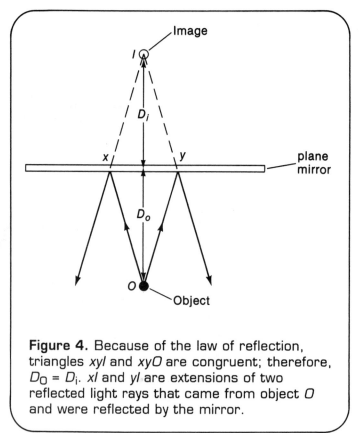

Figure 4. Because of the law of reflection, triangles xyI and xyO are congruent; therefore, $D_O = D_i$. xI and yI are extensions of two reflected light rays that came from object O and were reflected by the mirror.

lishes a relationship for the way light bends when it passes from one transparent medium to another, is not as easy to discover. It usually requires some hints because the relationship between the angle of incidence (usually in air) and the angle of refraction in another medium is not very obvious.

It is clear that light bends when it passes from water to air or vice versa. All you need do is place a pencil in a glass of water. When you look at it, you'll see that the pencil appears to be broken at the point where it enters the water. Light traveling from the pencil to your eye through air takes a different path than does light that travels through both water and air.

Here's another way to convince yourself that light bends. Place a coin on the bottom of a teacup. Then lower your head so that the coin just disappears from view, that is, so that the cup just interrupts your line of sight to the coin. Now have someone pour water into the cup, being careful not to disturb the coin. You'll find that the coin becomes visible again. Light from the coin bends as it passes from water to air as shown in Figure 5.

To look for the relationship between the angle of incidence, i, and the angle of refraction, rf, as shown in Figure 6, you'll need to measure these angles for a number of different values of i. To do this, place a large piece of white paper on a sheet of soft cardboard or a bulletin board laid flat on a table. Use a pin to scratch a vertical line down the exact middle of the flat side of a clear plastic semicircular box. Fill in the scratch with black ink so it will be easily seen. Fill the box with water and place it on the white paper. Draw a line around the bottom of the box so that you can put it

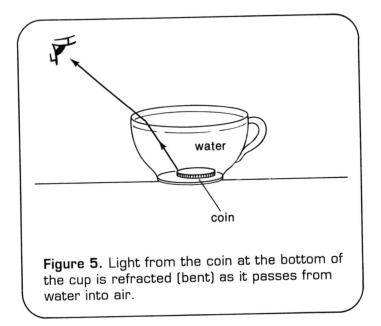

Figure 5. Light from the coin at the bottom of the cup is refracted (bent) as it passes from water into air.

back in the same place if you should accidentally move it. Make another mark on the paper directly beneath the bottom of the scratch.

Use a vertical pin and the vertical black scratch to define an incident light ray perpendicular to the surface of the box as shown in Figure 7. Since the angle of incidence is measured from the normal (the line perpendicular to the surface), the angle of incidence of this ray is 0°. Now look at the ray of light established by the pin and the scratch through the water from the curved side of the box. Move your eye until the pin and the scratch line up as seen through the water. Use another pin to mark this line of sight. How much is light refracted when it enters water at an angle of incidence of 0°?

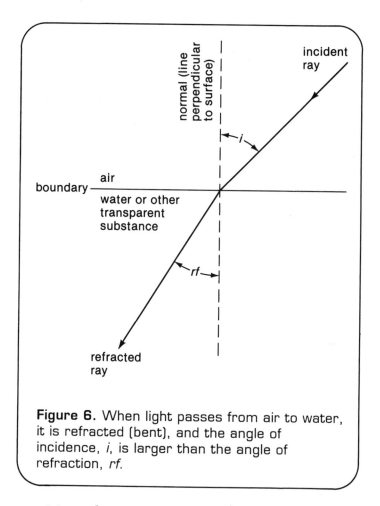

Figure 6. When light passes from air to water, it is refracted (bent), and the angle of incidence, *i*, is larger than the angle of refraction, *rf*.

Move the pin to a new position so that the angle of incidence is about 20° and repeat the experiment. Use the second pin as before to mark the refracted ray as seen through the water. Since refraction occurs at the midpoint of the flat side of the box, the refracted ray will lie along a radius of the box and will strike the curved side at 90° to a tangent drawn to that point. Therefore, it will

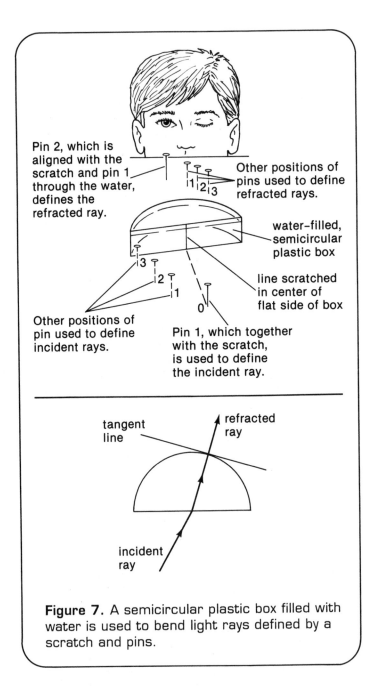

Pin 2, which is aligned with the scratch and pin 1 through the water, defines the refracted ray.

Other positions of pins used to define refracted rays.

water-filled, semicircular plastic box

line scratched in center of flat side of box

Other positions of pin used to define incident rays.

Pin 1, which together with the scratch, is used to define the incident ray.

tangent line

refracted ray

incident ray

Figure 7. A semicircular plastic box filled with water is used to bend light rays defined by a scratch and pins.

not be refracted a second time. See Figure 7 (inset). Continue to mark new incident and refracted rays, increasing the angle of incidence each time, until you are as close to 90° as viewing allows. By numbering the successive holes left by the two pins, you can identify the incident rays that match the corresponding refracted rays.

Carefully remove the semicircular box and use a ruler and pencil to mark the incident and refracted rays as shown in Figure 8. (Remember, you made a mark directly beneath the scratch that defined the end of the incident ray and the beginning of the refracted ray.) For each pair of rays—incident and refracted—that you made, use a protractor to measure angle i (the angle of incidence) and angle rf (the angle of refraction).

If you can't find a clear semicircular plastic box, place a narrow rectangular box filled with water or a solid glass or plastic block near the center of the paper. Draw a line along both sides of the box or block with a pencil so that you can put it back in the same place if you should accidentally move it.

You'll need two pins to establish an incident ray as shown in Figure 9. Now look at the pins through the glass, plastic, or water from the other side of the block or box. With two more pins, establish another ray of light that appears to be in line with the first ray. You can do this by aligning the second pair of pins with the first pair as you look at them through the transparent box or block as shown in Figure 9.

Remove the pins and write a little number "1" beside each of the four pinholes that are in the paper. In that way you'll be able to pair the incident rays and draw the corresponding refracted rays as you repeat the experiment a

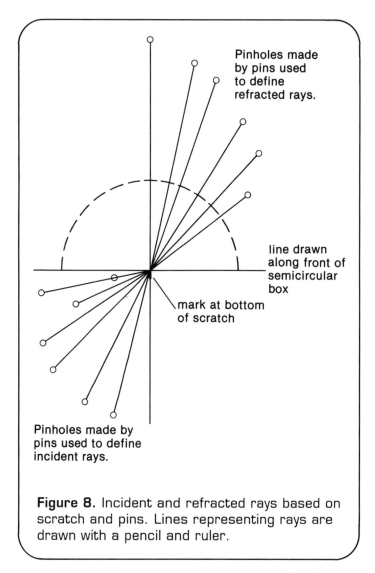

Pinholes made
by pins used
to define
refracted rays.

line drawn
along front of
semicircular
box

mark at bottom
of scratch

Pinholes made by
pins used to define
incident rays.

Figure 8. Incident and refracted rays based on scratch and pins. Lines representing rays are drawn with a pencil and ruler.

number of times to establish a variety of incident angles ranging from about 20° to 80°. The holes left by the pins used to mark the next set of rays can be marked with a "2," the next with a "3," and so on.

If you used the block or water-filled rect-

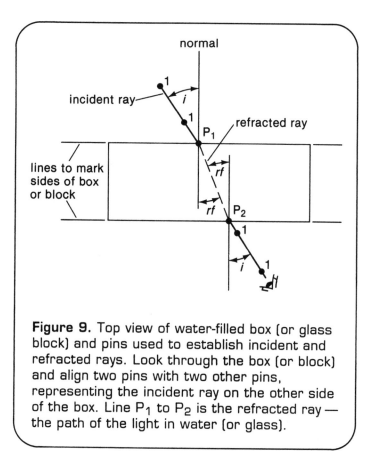

Figure 9. Top view of water-filled box (or glass block) and pins used to establish incident and refracted rays. Look through the box (or block) and align two pins with two other pins, representing the incident ray on the other side of the box. Line P_1 to P_2 is the refracted ray — the path of the light in water (or glass).

angular box, remove it and use a ruler to draw a line along each set of pinholes (rays) that you have made. Your drawing will look something like the one in Figure 10. For light to follow the parallel paths shown by the pairs of rays you've established, it must have traveled through the water along the dotted lines indicated in Figure 10. The angle between one of these dotted lines, which represent the refracted rays, and the normal (perpendicular) to the surface is the angle of refraction, *rf*. The angle between the normal and the incident ray that was bent to form the refracted ray is defined as the *angle of incidence.* Compare the incident angles on both sides of the box or block. They should be very nearly the same.

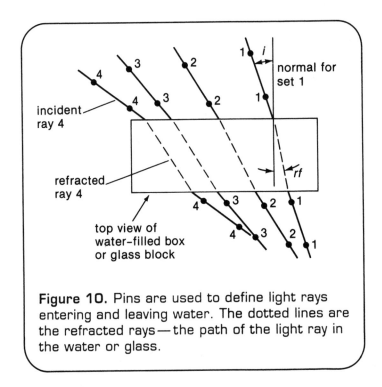

Figure 10. Pins are used to define light rays entering and leaving water. The dotted lines are the refracted rays—the path of the light ray in the water or glass.

Regardless of the method you used, which angle, *i* or *rf*, is bigger in each case? Is the ratio of the angles constant? To find out, plot a graph of ∠ *rf* vs. ∠ *i*. Does the graph indicate that ∠ *i* is proportional to ∠ *rf*: that is, is the graph a straight line? Does it appear to be straight for small angles of incidence?

Using a pocket calculator, or a table of sines, find the sine of each angle of incidence and the sines of the corresponding angles of refraction. Try plotting the sines of the angles of refraction (dependent variable) on the vertical axis and the sines of the corresponding angles of incidence (independent variable) on the horizontal axis. What do you find now?

You can see why some hints are needed to establish the law of refraction, which is known as *Snell's law*, namely, that the sine of the angle of incidence is proportional to the sine of the angle of refraction for light passing from air into another transparent medium. Snell's law is often written in the form

$$\frac{\sin i}{\sin r} = n$$

where angle *i* is measured in a vacuum (or air) and angle *r* in a medium such as glass, water, or diamond. The value of *n* for any particular material is a characteristic property known as the index of refraction for that substance. A table of refractive indices is given in Table 1.

Table 1: The Refractive Index of Some Substances

Substance	Index of refraction
water	1.33
fused quartz	1.46
oleic acid	1.46
glycerin	1.47
glass	1.5–1.9
diamond	2.42

THE INDEX OF REFRACTION
AND DENSITY

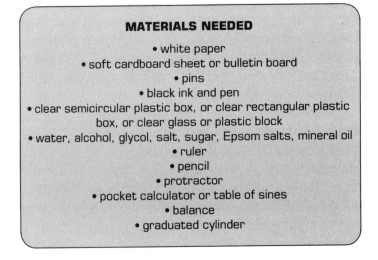

MATERIALS NEEDED

- white paper
- soft cardboard sheet or bulletin board
- pins
- black ink and pen
- clear semicircular plastic box, or clear rectangular plastic box, or clear glass or plastic block
- water, alcohol, glycol, salt, sugar, Epsom salts, mineral oil
- ruler
- pencil
- protractor
- pocket calculator or table of sines
- balance
- graduated cylinder

My students often assumed that the index of refraction of a transparent substance was directly proportional to the density of the material, which is its mass per unit volume. You can check up on their assumption by gathering together a number of transparent substances such as water, alcohol, mineral oil, glycol (antifreeze), a concentrated solution of sugar, and a concentrated solution of salt and/or Epsom salts, a glass block, and a plastic block. Measure the refractive index of each of these substances. Then determine their densities using a balance and a ruler or a graduated cylinder.

Once you have gathered all your data, plot a graph of the refractive index of a substance vs. its density. What do you conclude? Was my students' intuitive assumption correct?

If you found that the index of refraction is not proportional to density, you might check to see whether it's proportional to the molecular density—the number of molecules per unit volume—or to the square or cube root of the molecular density. To find the molecular density, you need to know the molecular mass of the substance and its density. For example, water (H_2O) has a molecular mass of 18 atomic mass units (2 + 16). This means that a mole of water (6.02×10^{23} molecules) has a mass of 18 grams. Since the density of water is 1.00 g/cm³, a mole of water occupies 18 cm³. The molecular density of water, therefore, is

$$\frac{6.02 \times 10^{23}}{18 \text{ cm}^3} = 3.3 \times 10^{22} \text{ molecules/cm}^3.$$

The mass of a mole of grain or ethyl alcohol is 46 g and its density is 0.79 g/cm³. Consequently, a mole of this alcohol has a volume of

$$\frac{46 \text{ g}}{0.79 \text{ g/cm}^3} = 58 \text{ cm}^3.$$

Its molecular density, therefore, is

$$\frac{6.02 \times 10^{23}}{58 \text{ cm}^3} = 1.0 \times 10^{22} \text{ molecules/cm}^3.$$

Can you find any reasonable mathematical relationship between molecular density and index of refraction? Between index of refraction and some other variable?

A CHANGING REFLECTED BEAM

This experiment is easy to do, but the results are surprising and difficult to explain, and this is where the challenge lies. Hold a small square or rectangular mirror so that it reflects sunlight onto a nearby wall or screen. What is the shape of the beam? Now look at the beam on a wall or screen that is about 100 meters (110 yards) away. What shape does the beam have at this distance?

Have someone use the mirror to reflect sunlight onto a screen that you move slowly away from the mirror. Keep your back to the mirror so that you **do not look directly into the beam.** Notice how the shape of the beam changes as you move farther from the mirror. Does the size of the beam change, too? Try to explain why the beam changes as it does as its distance from the mirror increases. Remember, each point on the spherical surface of the sun emits light that travels outward in all directions; each point on the mirror receives light from all points on the side of the sun that faces Earth.

A simple experiment with pinholes may also be helpful. Make a pinhole in a dark sheet of paper. Then hold the paper so that sunlight comes through the pinhole. If you hold a piece of white cardboard or some other white screen beyond the pinhole, the light that comes through the hole will form a pinhole image of the sun. Now use a sharp knife or scissors to cut tiny triangular or square holes in the dark paper. Examine the images of the sun formed when sunlight passes through these small holes. Is the sun's image still round?

DISAPPEARING SHADOWS

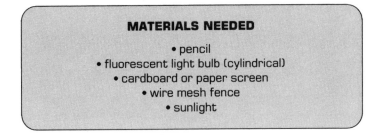

MATERIALS NEEDED

• pencil
• fluorescent light bulb (cylindrical)
• cardboard or paper screen
• wire mesh fence
• sunlight

I like this experiment because it reveals that some things we see every day, things as simple as shadows, raise questions that require some thoughtful analysis to figure out.

Hold a pencil in front of, and parallel to, the axis of a long cylindrical fluorescent light bulb. As you might expect, you will see a shadow of the pencil on a wall or a screen held behind the pencil.

Now turn the pencil so that its axis is perpendicular to the axis of the bulb. Why does the shadow of the pencil nearly disappear?

Stand near a wire mesh fence on a bright sunny day in late afternoon. The shadow of the bottom of the wire fence can be seen quite clearly on the ground near the fence. But look at the shadow of the top of the fence, which is farther away. Its shadow will be invisible, or fuzzy at best. Can you explain why the lower end of the fence's shadow is sharp while the upper end is nearly invisible?

Look at your own shadow near sunset. How does the shadow of your feet and ankles compare with that of your head? What causes the difference?

THE WAVELENGTH OF LIGHT

MATERIALS NEEDED

• showcase or other bulb that has a long, straight vertical filament
• diffraction grating
• scissors
• black construction paper
• 2 in × 2 in slide
• slide projector
• white screen or wall
• diffraction grating
• ruler

Although teenage students are often reluctant to acknowledge that learning can be exciting, most of mine had difficulty hiding the thrill they experienced in measuring something as small as the wavelength of light. As you may know, many properties of light can be explained by assuming that light behaves as if it were wavelike. When water waves pass through a narrow opening, they are diffracted; that is, they spread out. If the size of the opening is comparable to the wavelength, the wave pattern becomes semicircular, almost as if the waves were coming from a new source—the kind that arises when you dip your finger up and down repeatedly in a pan of water.

To see a similar effect with light, look at a light bulb, such as a showcase bulb that has a long vertical filament. Make the light pass through a narrow slit before it enters your eye. This can be done by squeezing your first two fingers almost together and looking at the filament, which should be a meter (yard) or more away, through this slit. You'll see the light spread out into bright

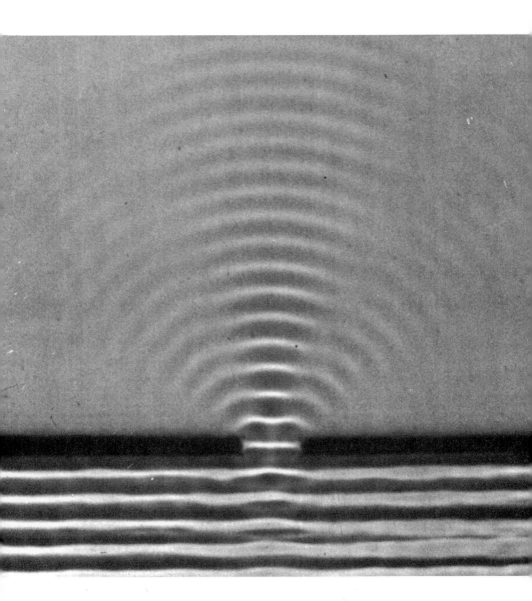

When straight water waves pass through a
narrow opening, they diffract (spread out). Notice
how the straight waves seen at the bottom of this
photo spread out into arc-shaped waves after
passing through a small opening in the barrier.

and dark bands. Do you see any color in the bands of light? You can create a similar effect by almost closing your eyes so that the light has to pass through the narrow openings between your eyelashes.

If periodic water waves are made to pass through two narrow openings that are close together, or if two wave sources produce waves simultaneously, a pattern such as that shown in the photograph on page 37 is formed. A drawing that explains this wave pattern is shown in Figure 11. Where crests or troughs of the waves coming from the two sources (S and S') overlap, the waves are higher or lower because the crests or troughs add together. Where the crest from one source overlaps the trough from the other, the waves cancel and the water remains undisturbed. At points where the *differences* in the distance to S and S' are $\frac{1}{2}$, $1\frac{1}{2}$, $2\frac{1}{2}$, $3\frac{1}{2}$ ... wavelengths the waves will cancel each other, forming the *nodal lines* that you see in the photograph and in Figure 11. A similar pattern will form if the waves pass through not two, but many, small equally spaced narrow openings.

Whether two or many slits are used, the nodal lines will be close together when the wavelength (λ) is small, and farther apart if the wavelength is larger. If the color of light is related to its wavelength, we might be able to separate the colors by having white light pass through openings that are very close together. Did you see any evidence that light could be separated into colors when you looked at light through a narrow opening?

If, in the pattern seen in Figure 11, you pick a

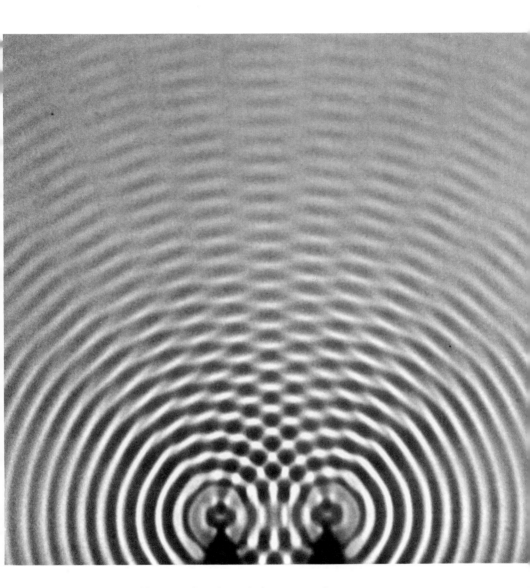

The overlapping of the waves from two wave
sources produces the pattern you see here.
It is called an interference pattern.
Notice how the waves cancel along lines,
called nodal lines, that extend outward
from between the two sources of waves.

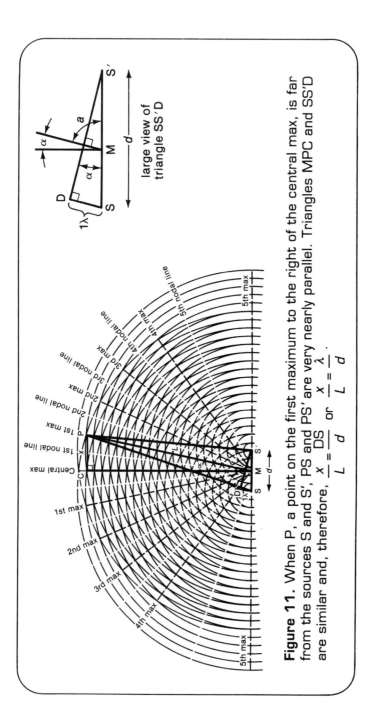

Figure 11. When P, a point on the first maximum to the right of the central max, is far from the sources S and S', PS and PS' are very nearly parallel. Triangles MPC and SS'D are similar and, therefore, $\dfrac{x}{L} = \dfrac{DS}{d}$ or $\dfrac{x}{L} = \dfrac{\lambda}{d}$.

point on the first maximum (along a line where crests fall on crests and troughs on troughs) to either side of the central maximum, the difference in the distance to the sources, S and S′, will be one wavelength (1 λ). If the point chosen is far from the sources, which are close together, the lines PS and PS′ will be very nearly parallel. The triangles MPC and SS′D are similar because both are right triangles and, since α + a = 90° and α′ + a = 90°, α′ = α. Because these triangles are similar, and because DS = 1 λ,

$$\frac{\lambda}{d} = \frac{x}{L}.$$

By measuring d, x, and L, we can calculate the wavelength λ because

$$\lambda = d\,\frac{x}{L}.$$

Since light is diffracted only when it passes through a very narrow opening, we know that the wavelength of light is very small. But if light forms a pattern like the ones seen in Figure 11 and the photograph, we might be able to measure d, x, and L without seeing the actual waves.

As you can see from the preceding equation, λ is proportional to the product of d and x and inversely proportional to L. Since we know λ is very small, we can expect the product of d and x to be small as well. But to determine x (the separation between the central maximum and the first maximum) the separation of the two maxima must be large enough to measure. One way to do that is to make d very small. What will this do to x? What should happen to the separation of the maxima, x, if we make L large?

A diffraction grating (which you can probably borrow from your school or buy from one of the science supply companies listed in the Appendix) has equally spaced lines that are very close together—just the kind of thing you need to diffract light into a visible pattern. The most common grating sold, which is quite inexpensive, has 5276 lines per centimeter (13,400/in). This means that d, the distance between the slits through which the light passes, can be easily determined.

$$d = \frac{1 \text{ cm}}{5276} = 0.00019 \text{ cm} \quad \text{or} \quad 1.9 \times 10^{-4} \text{ cm}.$$

Once you have such a diffraction grating, you can produce an interference pattern that will enable you to measure the wavelength of light. Standing several meters from the light you looked at before, look at it again with the grating in front of your eye. If the lines in the grating are parallel to the light filament, the light should be diffracted, and you will see rainbowlike spectra to either side of the light's filament. If you don't see them, rotate the grating 90° and look again.

These spectra, which appear to be out in space, are on the retina of your eye. Your brain automatically sees them spread out to either side of the position of the light. The fact that you see many colors suggests that the different colors in white light have different wavelengths. Since d, the distance between the slits in the grating, is the same for all the colors that pass through the grating and L is about the same, the differences in x for the various colors must be due to the wavelength, λ. According to the equation we developed previously, which color has the longest wavelength? The shortest wavelength?

Now, to measure the wavelength, use scissors to cut a narrow slit in a small piece of black film or construction paper. Place the paper in an empty 2 in × 2 in slide used in slide projectors. With the slit aligned vertically, place it in a slide projector. Focus the bright vertical beam on a white screen or wall about 50 cm (20 in) from the projector in a dark room. Tape the diffraction grating over the end of the tube that holds the projector's lens. The vertical beam of light must now pass through the grating. Be sure the grating spreads the light horizontally.

You should be able to see the first maxima about 10 cm to either side of the bright focused beam that constitutes the central maximum. Depending on how dark the room is, you may be able to see less intense maxima at greater distances to the side.

With this pattern in place, you're ready to make measurements that will enable you to calculate the wavelength of light of different colors. You already know the value of d if your grating has 13,400 lines per inch. You can measure x for violet light by using a ruler to measure the distance from the center of the central max to the innermost edge of the violet light in the spectrum on the screen. Measure to the spectrum on both sides and take an average. (It is difficult to align the beam so that it is exactly perpendicular to the screen.) You can find L by measuring the distance from the center of the grating to the edges of the violet light on both sides of the central max as shown in Figure 12, or by measuring x and b (the distance from the grating to the screen) and using the Pythagorean theorem $(x^2 + b^2 = L^2)$.

What do you calculate the wavelength of vio-

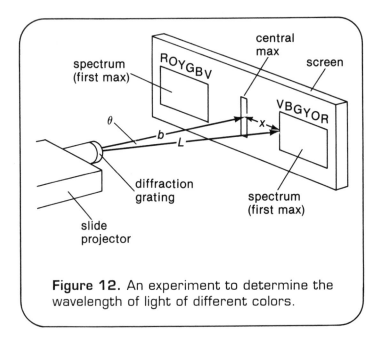

Figure 12. An experiment to determine the wavelength of light of different colors.

let light to be? What do you find is the longest wavelength of the red light you can see? What do you find is the average wavelength of green light? Of yellow light? Of blue light?

The equation $\lambda = d(x/L)$ is sometimes written $\lambda = d \sin \theta$, where θ is the angle shown in Figure 12. If you know a little trigonometry, explain why these two equations are equivalent.

The wavelengths of light are usually expressed in nanometers (1 nm = 10^{-9} m). How do your calculations for the wavelengths of light compare with the values given in Table 2?

Ask different people to look at the spectra on the screen and point out the deepest violet or red that they can see. Can some people see more of the spectrum than others? Can color-blind people see the entire spectrum? Can people who are red color-blind see the red portion of the spectrum? If so, what does it look like to them? How about people who are blue-green color-blind?

Table 2: The Wavelengths of the Colors of Light Seen in the Visible Spectrum

Color	Wavelength (nanometers)
violet	400–450
blue	450–500
green	500–570
yellow	570–590
orange	590–610
red	610–700

THE SIZES OF THE SUN AND MOON

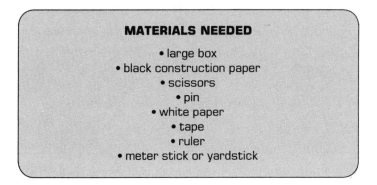

MATERIALS NEEDED

- large box
- black construction paper
- scissors
- pin
- white paper
- tape
- ruler
- meter stick or yardstick

Both the sun and the moon have a diameter of about 0.5 degree. That is, about 360 suns or moons placed side by side would stretch from the eastern to the western horizon. On the basis of their size alone and your experience in judging distance, if you didn't know better, you would probably guess that they are the same distance from the Earth. However, the sun is 150,000,000 km (94,000,000 mi) from the Earth, while the moon is only 380,000 km (240,000 mi). Knowing their distances and the fact that they appear to have about the same size, what would you estimate the ratio of their diameters to be?

You can check up on this ratio by doing experiments that will allow you actually to calculate their diameters. Since you should **never look directly at the sun,** you can measure its diameter by measuring a pinhole image of the sun as shown in Figure 13. When you are kneeling inside a large box with your back to the sun, the sunlight coming through a pinhole will provide a clear image that you can see and measure quite easily with a ruler. From the diameter of the image, d, the length of the box, L, and the known distance to the sun, L, you can calculate the sun's diameter, D.

Devise your own experiment to calculate the moon's diameter. What do you find the diameter of the moon to be? How does it compare with the sun? Earlier, you estimated the ratio of diameters of the sun and moon based on their relative distances from the Earth and their apparent equality of size. How does that earlier ratio compare with the one you just made?

This pattern of pinhole images of the sun, found within the shadow cast by a tree, is made when sunlight passes through the small openings between the leaves.

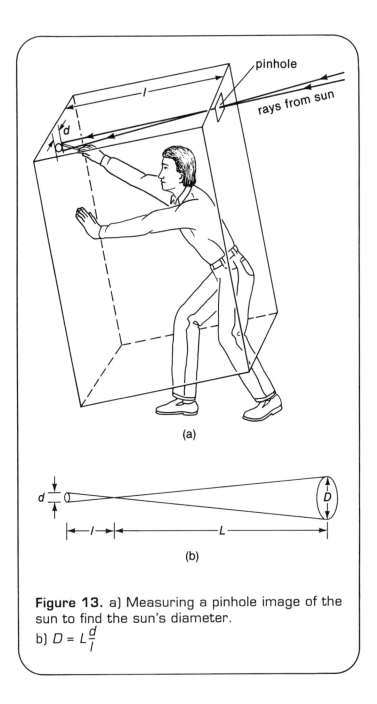

Figure 13. a) Measuring a pinhole image of the sun to find the sun's diameter.

b) $D = L\dfrac{d}{l}$

MAPPING THE SUN'S PATH
ACROSS THE SKY

MATERIALS NEEDED

• clear plastic dome or a large fine-mesh kitchen strainer
• heavy flat sheet of cardboard
• pen or pencil
• marking pen or round-headed pins
• yarn or string
• clear sunny day

Each day the sun appears to rise in the east, move slowly across the sky, and set in the west. During the early winter in the United States, the sun's path is quite short and close to the southern horizon. Its path changes slightly every day. By early summer, the sun follows a long path across the heavens. It rises in the northeast, reaches a point nearly overhead at midday, and sets in the northwest.

You should **never look directly at the sun** because it can damage your eyes, but you can use a clear plastic dome or a large fine-mesh kitchen strainer to make a map of the sun's path across the sky. If you do this at certain times of the year, you'll be able to determine the maximum and minimum heights reached by the sun at your latitude, its rising and setting points, and the variation in its motion relative to your position on the Earth. Simply place the dome or strainer on a heavy flat sheet of cardboard. Use a pen or pencil to mark the outline of its base on the cardboard. Then make a mark at the very center of the circle you have drawn. The mark represents your position relative to the domelike sky across which the sun will move. Put the dome back in position and tape it to the cardboard.

At sunrise, put the dome outside on a level surface in an open area where it will be in the sun all day. Fasten the cardboard firmly in position so that it cannot be moved. Use a marking pen (if you use a plastic dome) or round-headed pins (if you use a strainer) to map the sun's position in the sky frequently throughout the day. This can be done by moving the tip of the pen or the pinhead until its shadow falls on the mark you made at the center of the circle. Once the shadow falls on the center of the circle, make a mark with the pen or leave the pin in place.

How do you know the pen mark or pin is now along a line that connects the sun with the dot at the center of the circle? In this model, what represents the sky? What represents the sun? What represents you?

By sunset, you will have a clear map of the sun's path across the sky. By connecting the pen marks with a dotted line, or the pins with a piece of yarn or string, you will have a permanent record of the sun's path for that day.

Repeat this experiment at different times of the year. If possible do it once a month, but particularly near the twentieth of March, June, September, and December. When is the sun's path highest and longest? Shortest and lowest? When is the direction of sunrise due east and sunset due west? Where does the sun rise and set during the rest of the year? Figure out a way to measure the sun's highest altitude at midday. What is its lowest altitude at midday? How can you use a shadow to mark the direction that is due north?

Design your own demonstrations to show why the sun's path across the sky changes from season to season.

2

CHALLENGING EXPERIMENTS IN PHYSICS

There are lots of challenging experiments in physics, but I tried to select those that my students liked best and that required no expensive equipment. Many challenging experiments in physics also reveal the role that mathematics plays in science, so I factored that into my choices as well. I still had to leave out some excellent experiments, but I hope you'll enjoy the ones I selected.

PROJECTILE MOTION

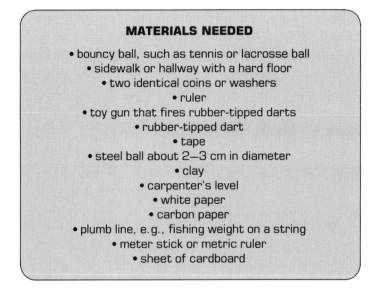

MATERIALS NEEDED

- bouncy ball, such as tennis or lacrosse ball
- sidewalk or hallway with a hard floor
- two identical coins or washers
- ruler
- toy gun that fires rubber-tipped darts
- rubber-tipped dart
- tape
- steel ball about 2–3 cm in diameter
- clay
- carpenter's level
- white paper
- carbon paper
- plumb line, e.g., fishing weight on a string
- meter stick or metric ruler
- sheet of cardboard

Four hundred years ago, Galileo showed the world that in the absence of air resistance the motion of a projectile, such as a ball fired from a cannon or thrown by an outfielder, can be considered as two independent motions: a vertical motion that depends only on gravity, and a horizontal motion that remains constant. You can demonstrate that Galileo is correct by doing a couple of simple experiments.

To show that the horizontal velocity of a projectile remains constant, drop a bouncy ball as you walk at a steady pace along a sidewalk or a hallway that has a hard floor. You'll find that you can continue to walk at the same velocity and catch the ball as it rebounds; you don't have to stop. Because you are carrying the ball when you drop it, it has the same velocity that you do. It retains that horizontal velocity as it falls and rebounds.

To show that an object moving horizontally falls with the same downward acceleration as an object that falls straight downward, try this: Put a coin or washer on the edge of a table or counter. Place an identical coin or washer on the end of a ruler that projects from the edge of the table as shown in Figure 14. Put your finger on the midpoint of the ruler, which should be near the edge of the table. With your other hand, hit the ruler sharply as shown. The coin near the edge of the table will fly out horizontally. The ruler will slide out from under the other coin, leaving it to fall straight down to the floor. Listen closely after you have hit the ruler. You'll hear both coins hit the floor at the same instant. What does this tell you? What else can you learn from this demonstration?

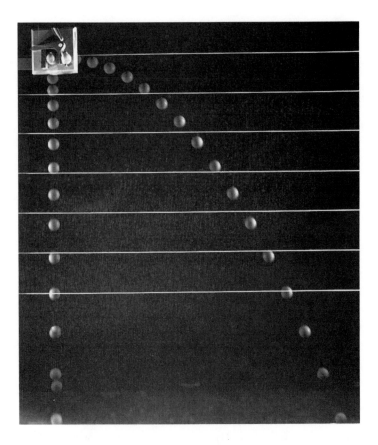

In this photo, one golf ball was projected horizontally at the same time that another was dropped. A flashing light in a dark room illuminated both golf balls every 1/30 of a second. The shutter of a camera focused on the balls was kept open for more than 0.5 seconds.

The white lines in the photograph were 0.15 m apart. Was the horizontal velocity of the projected ball constant? If so, what was its horizontal velocity? What is the acceleration of the dropped ball? From the picture, how can you tell that both balls had the same acceleration?

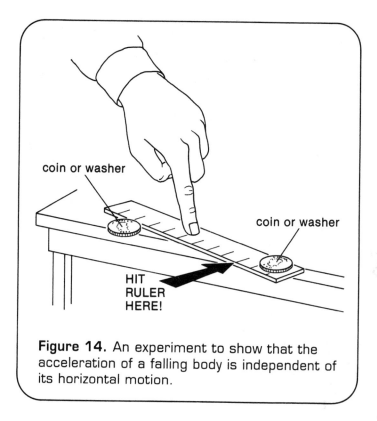

coin or washer

coin or washer

HIT
RULER
HERE!

Figure 14. An experiment to show that the acceleration of a falling body is independent of its horizontal motion.

Now, let's use what Galileo taught us to make some measurements and some predictions. You'll need a toy gun that fires firm rubber-tipped darts like the one shown in Figure 15. To reduce the range of the gun, tape a steel ball about 2–3 cm in diameter to the concave surface of the rubber-tipped end of the dart. Secure the gun to the edge of a table with clay, and use a carpenter's level to be sure that the barrel of the gun is level. Place a dart with the attached steel ball into the gun. **Be certain no one is in front of the gun.** Then fire the gun and note the approximate place where the dart hits the floor.

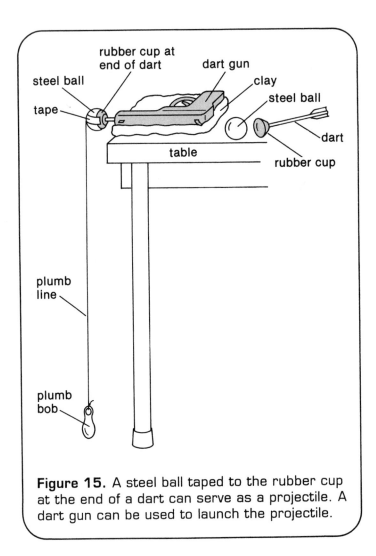

Figure 15. A steel ball taped to the rubber cup at the end of a dart can serve as a projectile. A dart gun can be used to launch the projectile.

Tape a sheet of white paper to the "landing zone" and cover it with a sheet of carbon paper. Fire the gun five or six more times to get an average range for the gun. The steel ball striking the carbon paper will leave distinct marks on the paper. Hang a plumb line, such as a fishing weight on a string, from the end of the gun to the floor. Then use a meter stick or metric ruler to measure the distance from the end of the lower end of the plumb line to the center of the five or six points on the paper. This will give you the horizontal distance the projectile traveled. To find the vertical distance that the projectile fell as it traveled horizontally, measure the distance from the end of the gun to the floor.

Since the vertical acceleration of an object falling near the surface of the Earth is 9.8 m/s² (10 m/s² is close enough for your purposes), you can calculate how long it took the ball to fall through the height, h, and reach the floor. The distance traveled by an object that accelerates uniformly is given by

$$d = \frac{1}{2} at^2.$$

In this case,

$$h = \frac{1}{2}(10 \text{ m/s}^2) \times t^2.$$

As you've seen, the vertical acceleration of the projectile is the same as if it fell straight downward to the floor. Therefore, if we know the height from the gun to the floor, we can calculate the time it took the projectile to reach the floor after it was fired. Suppose the height from floor to gun is 1 m; then the time to fall this distance is

$$t = \sqrt{\frac{2h}{10 \text{ m/s}^2}} = \sqrt{\frac{2 \times 1 \text{ m}}{10 \text{ m/s}^2}} = \sqrt{0.20 \text{ s}^2} = 0.45 \text{ s}.$$

Now that we know how long it took the projectile to reach the floor, we can determine what its horizontal velocity, vH, was because we know it traveled horizontally a distance, dH, and

$$V_H = \frac{d_H}{t}.$$

If the projectile traveled 1.8 m horizontally before it hit the floor, then its horizontal velocity can be determined:

$$V_H = \frac{d_H}{t} = \frac{1.8 \, m}{0.45 \, s} = 4.0 \, m/s.$$

With this information about the projectile, try to predict the height to which the projectile will rise if fired directly upward. Remember, the "bullet" will rise until its velocity becomes zero. If its muzzle velocity (the velocity it has when it leaves the gun) was 4.0 m/s, its change in velocity, Δv, will be −4.0 m/s. Since it will accelerate downward at 10 m/s² after being fired, the time it will take the projectile to reach its maximum height can be calculated:

$$\Delta v = at.$$

Using the previous example,

$$-4.0 \, m/s = -10 \, m/s^2 \times t.$$

Therefore, the time for the projectile to reach its maximum height can be calculated. In the example used,

$$t = \frac{-4.0 \text{ m/s}}{-10 \text{ m/s}^2} = 0.40 \text{ s.}$$

If the bullet maintained its velocity (say, 4.0 m/s), then it would rise to a height of 1.6 m (0.40 s × 4.0 m/s) in 0.40 s. But we know its velocity is decreasing at the rate of 10 m/s². Therefore, the height to which it actually rises is equal to the distance it would have gone, were there no acceleration, minus the height it loses as a result of its acceleration ($\frac{1}{2} at^2$). Figure 16 shows this graphically. In the example given, the height to which it will rise is

$h = vt - (\frac{1}{2} at^2)$
$\quad = (4.0 \text{ m/s} \times 0.40 \text{ s}) - [\frac{1}{2} \times 10 \text{ m/s}^2 \times (0.40 \text{ s})^2] = 0.80 \text{ m.}$

Predict the maximum height to which the projectile from your gun will rise if fired straight upward. Then test your prediction. Support a sheet of cardboard at the predicted height above the bullet. **With only the cardboard and its support above the gun,** fire the projectile from the gun. How close does it come to the height you predicted?

Use a protractor to make a giant protractor on a sheet of cardboard as shown in Figure 17. Predict the angle at which you should fire the projectile to give it its maximum horizontal range. (If you know something about vectors and trigonometry, you might even be able to predict how far the bullet will travel horizontally.) Then test your prediction by firing it at different angles. **Be sure no one is in front of the gun.** Be sure the steel-ball bullet is always the same height above

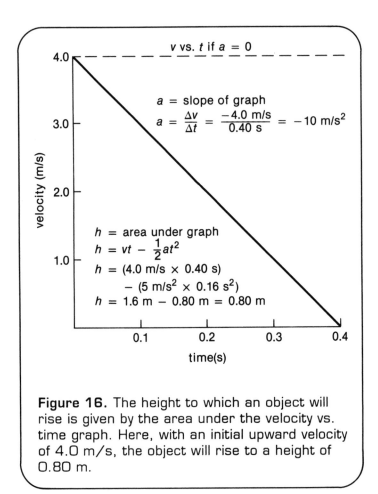

Figure 16. The height to which an object will rise is given by the area under the velocity vs. time graph. Here, with an initial upward velocity of 4.0 m/s, the object will rise to a height of 0.80 m.

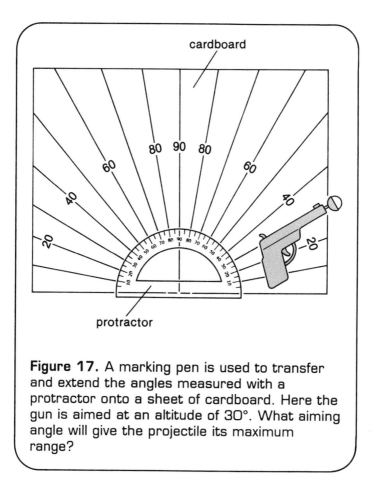

cardboard

80 90 80

60 60

40 40

20 20

protractor

Figure 17. A marking pen is used to transfer and extend the angles measured with a protractor onto a sheet of cardboard. Here the gun is aimed at an altitude of 30°. What aiming angle will give the projectile its maximum range?

the floor each time you fire. Was your prediction correct?

• Use what you have learned in this experiment to determine the approximate velocity of the water fired from a squirt gun.

HOOKE'S LAW AND MORE

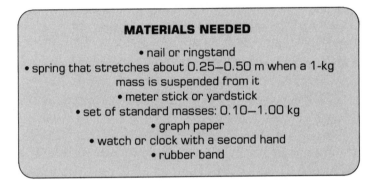

MATERIALS NEEDED

• nail or ringstand
• spring that stretches about 0.25–0.50 m when a 1-kg mass is suspended from it
• meter stick or yardstick
• set of standard masses: 0.10–1.00 kg
• graph paper
• watch or clock with a second hand
• rubber band

Robert Hooke, a contemporary of Newton, was probably the first to discover the law that bears his name. You can make the same discovery by carrying out the following experiment.

Hang a spring from a nail or some other firm means of support. (A screen door spring that stretches about 0.25–0.50 m when a 1-kg mass is hung on it is a good choice.)

Place a meter stick or yardstick behind the spring so you can measure the amount the spring is stretched (S) when various weights (W) are hung on its lower end. A set of standard masses from 0.10 to 1.00 kg will enable you to hang up to 1.5 kg on the spring. Since the masses are pulled by gravity with a force of 9.8 N/kg, a mass of 1.0 kg has a weight of 9.8 N (newtons). A mass of 0.50 kg weighs 4.9 N. How much does 0.10 kg weigh? 1.5 kg?

If you place the zero point of the meter stick so that it is even with the bottom of the spring, the stretch will simply be the new position of the bottom of the spring when a weight is added.

Once you've measured the stretch of the spring with masses from 0.20 to 1.5 kg suspended from it, remove the masses in the reverse order that they were added and measure the stretch again after each mass is removed. Do the values of stretch that you find for each mass as the spring contracts agree with the values you found when the masses were added?

After you've collected your data, plot a graph of the weight, W, hung on the spring (vertical axis) versus the stretch, S, of the spring (horizontal axis). What do you find about the relationship between the force applied to the spring and the amount the spring stretches? This relationship is known as Hooke's law.

• Another discovery made by Robert Hooke is related to the period of an oscillating spring. You may have noticed that the spring tends to oscillate up and down with a constant frequency if the weight is lifted a short distance and released. Hang a 1-kg mass on the lower end of a spring. Lift it a short distance and release it. Then determine the *period* of the spring: the time for the weight to make one complete oscillation, up and down. The best way to do this is to use a watch or clock with a second hand or mode and determine how long it takes the spring to make about a hundred oscillations. Then divide the total time by 100. Why is this better than timing one oscillation?

Now change the amplitude (size) of the oscillation by lifting the mass a little bit farther before releasing it. Does the period change with the amplitude? How is the period related to the *frequency of oscillation* (the number of times the mass moves up and down in each second)?

• Is the period of the oscillating spring related to the mass suspended from it? To find out, determine the period for masses ranging 0.20 kg to 1.5 kg. Plot a graph of the period vs. the mass suspended. Is the period proportional to the mass suspended from the spring? Is it proportional to the square root of the mass? How would the frequency of oscillation be related to the mass?

• The slope of the graph (weight/stretch) you made when you discovered Hooke's law is called the spring constant, k. What are the units of k? Using the graph of stretch versus weight that you made, determine how the work done on a spring is related to its stretch. If you don't already know, *work* is defined as the product of force and distance. However, in stretching a spring, the force required increases as the spring stretches; therefore, to find the total work done, you must find the area under the weight vs. stretch graph. How much work is done in stretching the spring 0.25 m? 0.50 m? The work done on the spring is stored as elastic potential energy in the spring. By virtue of its stretch, it has the capacity to do work on something else. For example, it could lift a weight. How is the energy stored in a stretched spring related to its stretch?

•   Find another spring that is more or less stiff than the spring you used before. What is the spring constant of this second spring? Is the period, T, of a spring related to its spring constant, k? Design an experiment to find out! Is T proportional to k? To $\sqrt{k}$? Is it proportional to the inverse of k? To $\sqrt{1/k}$?

•   Now that you know how the period, T, of a spring is related to the mass, m, suspended from it and to the spring constant, k, write an expression that relates all three of these variables—T, m, and k. What is the proportionality constant for this expression?

•   In the last experiment, you may have found at some point that a particular mass caused the spring's motion to alternate between a bouncing up-and-down motion and a swinging to-and-fro motion. If not, try hanging various masses on the spring until you find such a mass. Then see whether you can figure out why the spring alternates between these two forms of motion when the "critical mass" is attached to it.

•   Repeat the Hooke's law experiment using a rubber band in place of the spring. Wait about 2 minutes before recording the final stretch for each mass you add to be certain you record the maximum stretch. Does a stretched rubber band follow Hooke's law? What is the stretch limit of the rubber band you used?

•   Again, add masses to a rubber band as you did before, but be careful this time not to exceed the stretch limit. Now remove the masses in the reverse order that they were added and measure the stretch again after each mass is removed. Do the values of stretch that you find for each mass as the rubber band contracts agree with the values you found when the masses were added to stretch the rubber?

On the same set of axes, plot a graph of stretch vs. force for the addition of weights to the rubber band and another for the stretch vs. force as the weights are removed. As you can see, the graphs do not agree. What does the area between the two graphs represent? How does the graph help you explain the fact that a rubber band becomes warm when it contracts?

ELASTIC AND GRAVITATIONAL POTENTIAL ENERGY

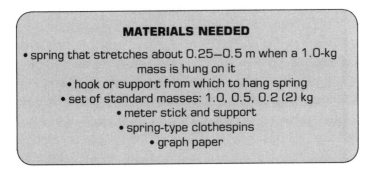

MATERIALS NEEDED

- spring that stretches about 0.25–0.5 m when a 1.0-kg mass is hung on it
- hook or support from which to hang spring
- set of standard masses: 1.0, 0.5, 0.2 (2) kg
- meter stick and support
- spring-type clothespins
- graph paper

A 1.0-kilogram mass 1 meter above a floor has a potential energy, relative to the floor, of about 10 joules (J). The potential energy is called *gravitational* potential energy because it exists as a result of the force of gravity. The mass is pulled toward the earth by a gravitational force of about 10 N because the Earth exerts a force of very nearly 10 N/kg (actually it's 9.8 N/kg) on all masses near its surface. Thus the force due to gravity on 1.0 kg is given by

$$1.0 \text{ kg} \times 10 \text{ N/kg} = 10 \text{ N}.$$

For a 2.0-kg mass, the force is given by

$$2.0 \text{ kg} \times 10 \text{ N/kg} = 20 \text{ N}.$$

If a 1-kg mass falls to the floor from a height of 1.0 m, the work done on it by the Earth will be

$$10 \text{ N} \times 1.0 \text{ m} = 10 \text{ J}.$$

Work is defined as the product of force and the distance through which the force acts. (This simple definition applies only when the force is in the same direction as the motion. If the force and motion are not parallel, only the component of the force along the motion contributes to the work.)

In the preceding example, the potential energy stored in the mass can be found from its potential to do work, which is equal to

$$F \times d \quad \text{or} \quad m \times 10 \text{ N/kg} \times h,$$

where h is the height above the floor—the distance through which the force of gravity can act. This potential energy is often expressed as mgh, where g is 10 N/kg—the force per mass with which the Earth pulls all masses near its surface.

If the 1.0-kg mass falls 1.0 m, its potential energy can be converted to 10 J of kinetic (motion) energy. The farther it falls, the more potential energy it loses and the more kinetic energy it acquires as its velocity grows. When it reaches the floor, the kinetic energy will be transformed into thermal energy (heat). The collision of the mass with the floor will increase the velocity of the molecules in the floor and in the mass. But what will happen if the mass is attached to a spring before it is released?

To find out, attach the upper end of the spring you've used before to a rigid support such as a hook that extends from a wall or a tall ring stand. Connect the 1.0-kg mass to the lower end of the spring, which has a meter stick behind it. Continue to hold the mass so that the spring remains *unstretched*. Then, being certain that the spring is *not* stretched, suddenly release the mass. What happens to the spring as the mass falls? What happens after the mass stops falling?

To find out how much the spring is stretched by the falling mass, mark the initial position of the lower end of the unstretched spring and the final position of the lower end of the spring when the mass reaches its lowest position with a pair of clothespins as shown in Figure 18. To do this, you will need two people: one to release the mass and the other to mark the final position of the lower end of the spring. You will probably have to repeat the experiment several times to find the exact final position of the spring as it is stretched by the falling mass. **Be careful: the falling mass packs quite a wallop!**

How much gravitational potential energy did the mass lose as it fell? Do you think the energy disappeared, or was it transformed into another form or forms of energy?

Suppose at the bottom of its fall the gravitational potential energy lost by the mass is stored as potential energy in the spring, which we'll call *elastic* potential energy. If this is the case, to what height should the mass rise on its return trip?

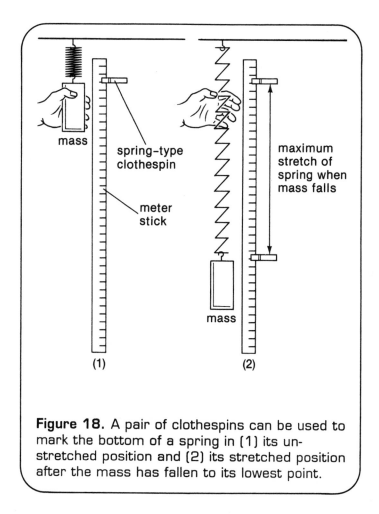

Figure 18. A pair of clothespins can be used to mark the bottom of a spring in (1) its un-stretched position and (2) its stretched position after the mass has fallen to its lowest point.

As you can see, the mass does rise to very nearly its original position. What does this tell you about the gravitational potential energy that was lost when the mass fell?

How much does the spring stretch when you let masses of 0.70 kg, 0.50 kg, 0.40 kg, and 0.20 kg fall while attached to the unstretched spring in the same way that the 1.0-kg mass was? Record this data and plot a graph of the elastic potential energy, in joules, stored in the spring vs. the stretch of the spring, in meters. You may assume that all the gravitational potential energy lost was transformed into elastic potential energy when the mass was at its lowest position. What basis do you have for making such an assumption?

Is the elastic potential energy stored in the spring proportional to the spring's stretch? If not, try plotting the elastic potential energy vs. the spring's stretch *squared*, that is, S^2. What do you find? If elastic potential energy $= kS^2$, what is the value of k? What units does it have?

• As the mass falls while attached to the spring, its gravitational potential energy decreases and the elastic potential energy stored in the spring increases. But between the top and bottom of its fall, the mass, m, moves; therefore it has kinetic energy ($\frac{1}{2} mv^2$). How can you determine what fraction of the gravitational energy lost is in the form of kinetic energy and what fraction is in the form of elastic potential energy at each point in its fall?

• When an object falls *freely*, its gravitational potential energy (mgh) changes to kinetic energy ($\frac{1}{2} mv^2$). Design an experiment to show that the kinetic energy gained by the object as it falls is equal to the potential energy it has lost.

BOYLE'S LAW AND AIR PRESSURE

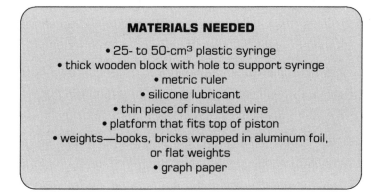

MATERIALS NEEDED

• 25- to 50-cm³ plastic syringe
• thick wooden block with hole to support syringe
• metric ruler
• silicone lubricant
• thin piece of insulated wire
• platform that fits top of piston
• weights—books, bricks wrapped in aluminum foil,
or flat weights
• graph paper

During the seventeenth century, Robert Boyle discovered a law of nature that still bears his name. In this experiment, you'll not only share his discovery, but see how the data leading to your discovery can be used to determine the pressure of the atmosphere.

Seal or plug the narrow end of a 25- to 50-cm³ plastic syringe like the one shown in Figure 19. If you don't have such a syringe, you may be able to borrow one from your school, or order one from one of the science supply houses listed in the Appendix. A thick wooden block with a hole drilled in it can be used to support the syringe. The diameter of the hole should match that of the syringe's cylinder.

What is the *inside* diameter of the cylinder? What is its cross-sectional area?

Add a little silicone lubricant to the rubber rings of the syringe's piston so it will slide easily in the cylinder. To make the piston stay at a fixed position in the cylinder, you can use a thin piece of insulated wire. Hold the wire in the cylinder

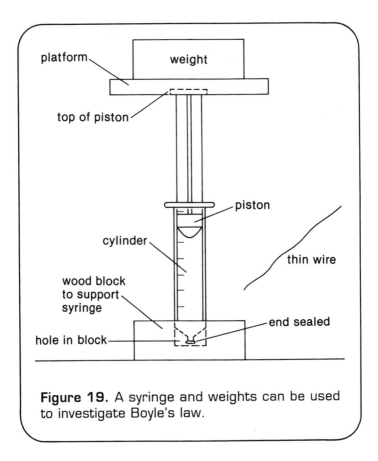

Figure 19. A syringe and weights can be used to investigate Boyle's law.

while you insert the piston. The tiny opening around the wire will allow air to escape as the piston is inserted. Set the lower ring of the piston near one of the upper markings on the cylinder. Remove the wire, rotate the piston, and press it downward to spread the lubricant. Notice how the piston springs back when pushed downward. Boyle referred to this as the "springiness" of air. Record the initial volume of the air trapped in the cylinder.

Now add weights (up to 50 N) to a platform that fits over the top of the piston to increase the force on the trapped gas. The gas, of course, exerts a force in the opposite direction. Books, bricks wrapped in aluminum foil, or flat weights can be used to apply force to the piston. Remember, 1.0 kg weighs approximately 10 N. (It actually weighs 9.8 N, but 10 N is only a 2 percent error.) Have a partner use his or her hands to guide the weights from the side as you add them. Record the volume of gas for each weight that rests on the piston. Then remove the weights and again record the volume for each weight. Your data table will look something like the following table:

Force (N)	Volume while adding weight (cm³)	Volume while removing weight (cm³)	Pressure (N/cm²)	1/Volume (1/cm³)
0	29.5	29.2		
10	19.9	19.7		
20	16.9	16.7		
40	14.8	14.7		
50	13.4	13.4		

Friction will retard the piston a little both on the way down and on the way up so you should probably take the average position as a measurement of the volume. When the piston is not moving, the pressure on both sides of it must be equal; that is, the pressure exerted by the gas equals the pressure exerted on it. To find the *pressure*, which is force per area, you can divide the force, in newtons, by the cross-sectional area of the cylinder, in square centimeters.

Convert your force readings to pressures and record them in your data table. Is the pressure of the gas really zero when there are no weights on the piston? Before you answer, consider what would happen to the piston if you took the syringe for a ride in an airplane or carried it to the top of a tall mountain.

Plot a graph of volume vs. pressure. What can you conclude? Try plotting the inverse of the volume, $1/V$ (vertical axis), vs. pressure (horizontal axis). What can you conclude from this graph?

When the pressure on a gas is zero, it occupies an infinite volume. Why? At infinite volume, $1/V \approx 0$. Why? Where is $1/V = 0$ on your graph?

Extrapolate (extend) your graph to the pressure axis where $(1/V) = 0$. What does the intercept of the line with the pressure axis represent? What would be the reading on a barometer when $(1/V) = 0$? How can you use your graph to determine air pressure? Atmospheric pressure at sea level is about 1.0×10^5 N/m². What is this pressure in N/cm²? In millimeters (mm) of mercury? How does it compare with the air pressure you determined using your graph?

Was it reasonable in your experiment to ignore the weight of the platform and piston?

A BALLISTIC PENDULUM TO MEASURE THE VELOCITY OF A WATER "BULLET"

When I taught physics, I liked to use a ballistic pendulum experiment as a way of reviewing many fundamental ideas while presenting an experiment that students found exciting. I did the experiment as a demonstration using a big

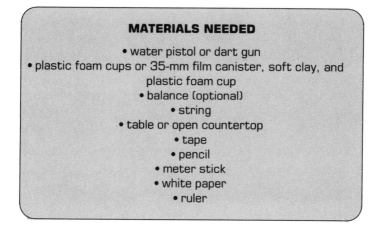

wooden block suspended from the ceiling. I fired a bullet from a .22-caliber rifle into the block after being certain that all my students were behind me. I'd be in real trouble if I suggested that you use a gun, so I found a way to do the experiment with a water pistol or a dart gun.

With a water pistol, you can fire a water "bullet" into some water in a plastic foam cup that is suspended as a pendulum bob. By measuring the bob's movement, you'll be able to determine the kinetic energy and momentum of the bullet. These values can then be used to find the bullet's velocity.

To begin, pour about 75 mL (75 g) of water into a plastic foam cup. The cup probably weighs about 2–3 g, but you can ignore it if you wish. (If you have a balance, you can weigh the cup and the water together.) Use a long piece of string to suspend the cup from a table or open countertop as shown in Figure 20a. With tape, it's easy to fasten the strings to the table or counter. A pencil can be used to punch holes in the side of the cup. When

Bullets travel at about the speed of sound or faster. How long could the shutter have been open on the camera used to take this picture?

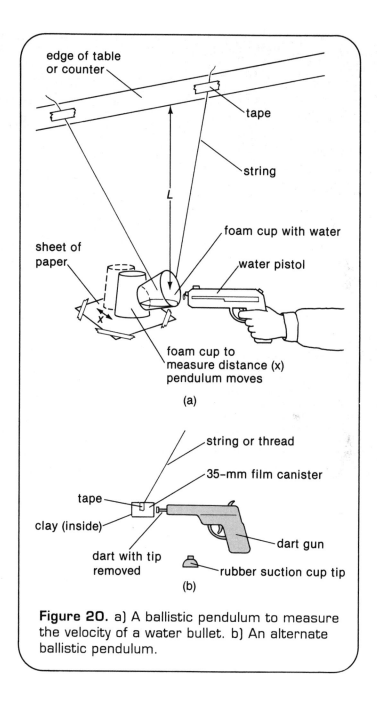

Figure 20. a) A ballistic pendulum to measure the velocity of a water bullet. b) An alternate ballistic pendulum.

suspended, the cup should be very close to the floor and tipped as shown so that you can fire the water bullet horizontally onto the upper surface of the water in the cup. Spreading the support strings adds stability to the pendulum and makes it swing straighter. To find the length, L, shown in the figure, use a meter stick to measure from the center of the cup to the bottom of the tabletop where the string is fastened.

Put a sheet of smooth white paper beneath the water-filled bob and tape it in place. Place a second, inverted, plastic foam cup behind the bob on the paper. It should just touch the bob, which should be completely at rest. Use a pencil to make a mark on the paper along the rear edge of the cup. Fire a single water "bullet" into the cup. The bob will move, displacing the cup behind it. Make a new mark along the rear edge of the cup at its new position. Then remove the inverted cup and measure the distance it moved.

Alternatively, as shown in Figure 20b, you can use a 35-mm film canister half-filled with a known mass of soft clay as a bob and a dart gun that fires darts with rubber suction-cup tips. To make the dart stick to the clay into which it will be fired, remove the rubber suction-cup tip from the dart before you load the gun. **Wear safety glasses and be sure no one is nearby.** Support the gun in a horizontal position close to the open end of the clay-filled film canister. Fire the dart into the center of the clay so that the bob and bullet move smoothly and without wiggling after they join.

The distance that the water- or clay-filled bob moves can be used to calculate the vertical height to which it rose. See Figure 21. Because the distance the cup moved (x in the diagram) is small compared with L, h will be small too. From the Pythagorean theorem, $(L - h)^2 + x^2 = L^2$. Therefore,

$$L^2 - 2Lh + h^2 + x^2 = L^2.$$

Since h is small, h^2 will be insignificant and can be dropped from the equation, leaving us with $L^2 - 2Lh + x^2 = L^2$. Subtracting L^2 from the equation and solving for h gives us

$$h = \frac{x^2}{2L}.$$

From your measurements of x and L, to what vertical height did the pendulum bob rise when struck by the water bullet or dart?

How much gravitational potential energy did the bob acquire? From the law of conservation of energy, the kinetic energy ($\frac{1}{2} mv^2$) acquired by the bob, which was free to move, must be very nearly equal to the potential energy that you calculated. Since you know the kinetic energy and the mass of the bob, you can determine its momentum, mv.

Momentum is conserved, even when energy is transformed from one form to another; therefore, the momentum of the water or dart bullet must be equal to the momentum of the bob and "bullet" after the bullet hit the cup. How can you find the mass of a single bullet fired from the gun?

Use the momentum and mass of the bullet to calculate the velocity of the bullet. What was the velocity of the bullet before it struck the bob?

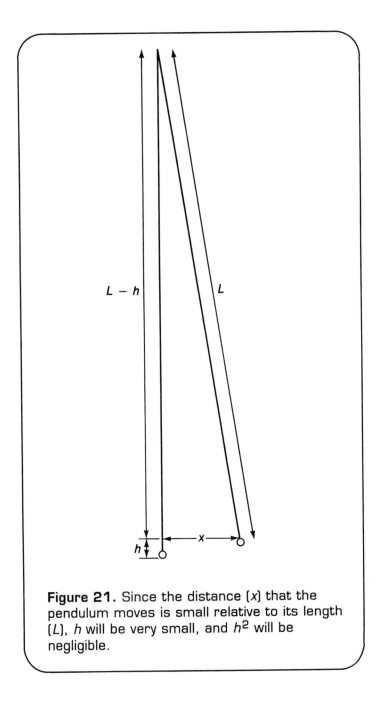

Figure 21. Since the distance (x) that the pendulum moves is small relative to its length (L), h will be very small, and h^2 will be negligible.

Now that you know the mass and velocity of the bullet, you can calculate the kinetic energy that it had *before* it struck the cup. What was its kinetic energy?

Collisions between objects are said to be elastic if no kinetic energy is lost in the collision. Collisions between gas molecules are normally elastic and billiard ball collisions are very nearly elastic. Collisions in which all or most of the kinetic energy is lost, such as when a ball of clay collides with a wall, are said to be inelastic. Was the collision between the bullet and the water- or clay-filled bob an elastic or an inelastic collision?

If the bullet were fired horizontally from a height of 1.0 m, how far would you expect it to travel? **Be sure that no one is nearby** before you fire the water or dart bullet. How far does it actually travel? The distance that you've measured is probably less than the distance you calculated. Why?

PHYSICS AT AN AMUSEMENT PARK

MATERIALS NEEDED

- accelerometer
- stopwatch or watch with second hand
- price of admission

If you go to an amusement park armed with an accelerometer (see Figure 22) and a stopwatch or a watch with a second hand or mode, you can investigate the physics associated with each ride and have a lot of fun at the same time.

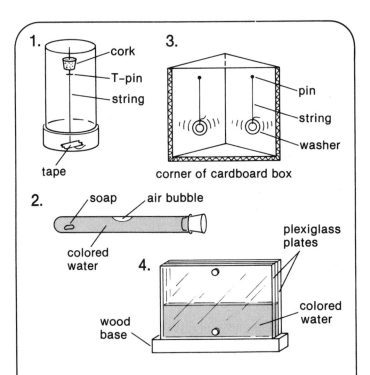

1.
cork
T-pin
string
tape

3.
pin
string
washer
corner of cardboard box

2.
soap
air bubble
colored water

4.
plexiglass plates
colored water
wood base

Figure 22. These accelerometers indicate the direction in which they are accelerated. The degree of movement of the indicator provides a rough measurement of the magnitude of the acceleration. Be sure to keep all accelero-meters level. 1. Plastic water-filled jar (inverted)–cork indicator connected by T-pin, thread, and tape to cover. Cork will move in direction of acceleration. 2. Test tube nearly filled with colored water and small piece of soap (to reduce surface tension)–air bubble moves in direction of acceleration. 3. Corner of cardboard box–washer moves in direction opposite that of the acceleration. 4. Two plexiglass plates with narrow, sealed space between them–low-water side indicates ("points to") direction of acceleration.

- Take your accelerometer on the merry-go-round. Where should you ride to obtain the largest reading on your accelerometer? Use your watch to determine the period of the merry-go-round and estimate the radius at the point where you are riding. From these measurements, determine the centripetal force acting on you.

- Take a ride on the swings that move in a circle. Explain why you swing outward at an angle as the swings begin to move. Why does the angle increase as you move faster? Regardless of your speed, why are all the swings, even the empty ones, at the same angle?

- If you're riding the rotor or spinning barrel, why do you "stick" to the wall once the rotation reaches a high frequency? In some of these rides, the floor falls away once you reach a certain speed. How must the force of friction compare to your weight if you are stuck to the wall? From the diameter of the rotor or barrel and its rate of rotation, calculate the centripetal force acting on you.

- If there is a ride that does a loop so that you are upside down at the top of the loop, compare how heavy you feel at the top and bottom of the loop. How can you explain the difference in the way you feel. Estimate the diameter of the loop. Then calculate the minimum speed that the loop-the-loop vehicle can have at the top of the loop.

- On which rides is potential energy transformed into kinetic energy? Estimate the magnitude of both kinds of energy. On which rides do you experience an increase in momentum? Since momentum is conserved, what is losing momentum as you gain it?

•   What other principles of physics can you find at the amusement park? What additional measurements can you make to demonstrate these principles?

THE SPEED OF SOUND

MATERIALS NEEDED

• two small boards or clicker ("cricket")
• large metal, concrete, or brick wall with open space nearby
• long measuring tape
• stopwatch
• thermometer

If from a distance of half a kilometer (0.31 mi) you watch a carpenter hit a nail, it's obvious that light travels much faster than sound. You hear the thump of the hammer about 1.5 seconds after you see the hammer strike. Assuming that light from the hammer reaches your eye instantaneously, the speed of sound must be approximately 330 m/s since

$$\frac{500 \text{ m}}{1.5 \text{ s}} = 330 \text{ m/s}.$$

The speed of light is not infinite, but it is so large (300,000 km/s or 186,000 mi/s) that it is difficult to measure it directly without rather sophisticated equipment. On the other hand, the speed of sound can be measured with very simple equipment.

The experiment described here to measure

the speed of sound in air is believed to be one that Newton performed more than 300 years ago. If this is done with care, the speed obtained is in good agreement with values obtained using considerably more expensive apparatus. It is similar to the carpenter-and-hammer experiment described previously, but the accuracy is improved by increasing the time interval.

If you clap together two small boards or snap a clicker (sometimes called a "cricket") while standing about 60–70 m (200–230 ft) from a large metal, concrete, or brick wall, you will hear the sound's echo a fraction of a second later. You might have a friend make the sound while you use a stopwatch to measure the time delay for the sound to travel 120–140 m to the wall and back. The variation in your stopwatch readings will convince you that the time interval is too short to measure with accuracy. However, you can improve the experimental accuracy by having your friend adjust the clapping or clicking rate until each clap or click coincides with the echo of the sound that preceded it. How can you be sure the sound is not being reflected from some reflecting surface other than the wall in front of you?

Once your partner has established the proper "rhythm" so that sound making and echoes coincide, you can start the stopwatch and count the number of sounds your partner makes over a period of 20 seconds or so. The time between claps is the time it takes the sound to travel to the wall and back to your ear. If you are 70 m from the wall, each clap represents a distance of 140 m (2 × 70 m) that the sound has traveled. If you counted 50 claps in 20 seconds, the time for the sound to travel 140 m was

$$\frac{20.0 \text{ s}}{50} = 0.40 \text{ s}.$$

How can you use this information to calculate the speed at which the sound traveled?

What do you find the speed of sound to be according to your measurements? Repeat the experiment several times. By what percentage do your measurements of the speed differ? Does this variation seem reasonable in view of the accuracy of your watch and the coincidence of sounds and echoes?

- Design an experiment to find out whether the speed of sound varies with the distance it travels. Does sound, like a runner, decrease its speed as the distance increases?
- What can you do to see whether the temperature of the air has any effect on the speed with which sound travels through it? Could you use the speed of sound to measure air temperature?
- Design an experiment to measure the speed of sound in a different medium. For example, how can you find the speed of sound in water?
- An approach similar to the one in this experiment has been used to measure the speed of light, but to do so requires much greater distances and/or a means of measuring much smaller intervals of time. If possible, assemble the equipment you need and measure the speed of light.

3

CHALLENGING HEAT EXPERIMENTS

The subject of heat is often taught in physics, chemistry, biology, and other disciplines because it is required to understand all of them. Because of its wide application and importance, I decided to devote a chapter to heat, but you will see references made to it in all the chapters, particularly in Chapter 4.

HEAT AND TEMPERATURE

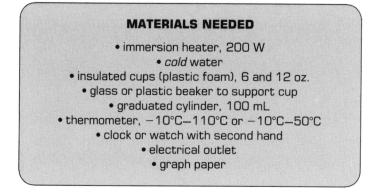

MATERIALS NEEDED

- immersion heater, 200 W
- *cold* water
- insulated cups (plastic foam), 6 and 12 oz.
- glass or plastic beaker to support cup
- graduated cylinder, 100 mL
- thermometer, −10°C–110°C or −10°C–50°C
- clock or watch with second hand
- electrical outlet
- graph paper

Many adults, as well as students, confuse heat and temperature. It's easy enough to say that the temperature of a body is a measure of the average kinetic energy of its molecules, while heat is the energy transferred between two objects because of a difference in their temperature. (The heat is always transferred from the warmer to the cooler object.) But saying and understanding are two different kettles of fish.

Early scientists thought of heat as an invisible fluid, called caloric, that flowed from warm objects to cooler ones. Fuels, such as wood and coal, were believed to be chemically combined with caloric so that the heat fluid was stored in the fuel. When the fuel burned, the caloric was released.

Today, the heat that early scientists viewed as something stored in matter is called *thermal energy*. It is the random kinetic (motion) energy of the atoms and molecules that make up a sample of matter. The faster the molecules move, the more kinetic energy they have. In fact, the kinetic energy of a single molecule, like the kinetic energy of any object, is equal to one-half its mass times its velocity squared ($E_K = \frac{1}{2}mv^2$). The average kinetic energy of the molecules of a body is proportional to the body's temperature. But the *total* thermal energy of the body depends on the number of molecules. Thus, a small object may have a high temperature, but little thermal energy. A large object, on the other hand, may have a low temperature but lots of thermal energy because it has many molecules.

The most practical way to see the difference between heat and temperature is do an experiment in which you transfer fixed amounts of heat to different masses of water and measure the temperature changes of the water. To begin, let's make an assumption. (Assumptions are very common in science and play a very useful role as long as you recognize that the assumption could be wrong.) We'll assume that the heat transferred to cold water by an immersion heater (which changes electrical energy to thermal energy) is proportional to the time the heater operates. It seems reasonable to assume that the heater will produce twice as much heat in 2 minutes as it does in 1 minute. Early scientists made the same assumption about candles and stoves. We'll define one blob of heat to be the amount of heat that your immersion heater delivers in 30 seconds.

To check up on the consistency of your heater, place 100 grams (g) of *cold* water in a 6-ounce insulated cup that is supported by a slightly larger glass or plastic beaker as shown in Figure 23. (Since the density of water is 1.0 g/mL, you can obtain 100 g by measuring out 100 mL in a graduated cylinder.) Use a thermometer to stir the water and measure its initial temperature. Then put the immersion heater in the water and plug it into an electrical outlet for exactly 30 seconds. **Never plug in the heater unless the coil is in water! And always grip the plug, *not* the cord, when disconnecting the heater.** After disconnecting the immersion heater, use it to stir the water. Do not remove the heater from the water until the water reaches its maximum temperature because it takes a few seconds for the heat to be transferred from the heater to the water. What was the temperature change of the water?

Repeat the experiment using another 100-g sample of cold water. Since your thermometers probably have a precision of $\pm1°$, how closely should the temperature change for the two experiments compare if the heater consistently delivers

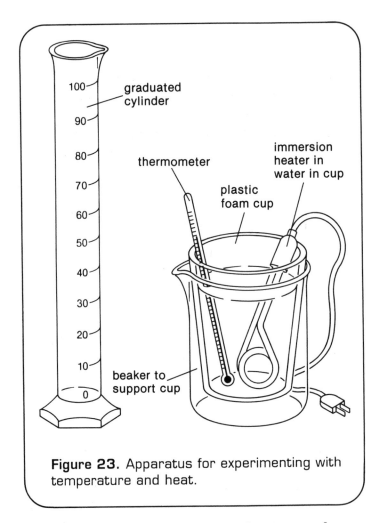

Figure 23. Apparatus for experimenting with temperature and heat.

one blob of heat every 30 seconds? Is your heater reasonably consistent? Why should you start with fresh samples of cold water every time you do the experiment?

Do you think the amount of heat transferred to the water will be proportional to the water's temperature change? To find out, add one blob of heat to 300 g of cold water in a 12-ounce insulated cup and measure the change in temperature of the water. (Remember, one blob of heat comes from having the immersion heater plugged in for 30 s.) Repeat the experiment, but this time add two blobs of heat to the 300 g of cold water. Then, in another trial, add three blobs of heat, and, finally, four blobs of heat to 300 g of cold water. Record your data in a table similar to the following one.

Some sample data for an immersion heater that I used in one trial is shown. T stands for temperature, which was measured in degrees Celsius (°C). If you use a Fahrenheit thermometer, you'll record the temperature in °F. The symbol Δ (delta) means "change in." In this case, it is the change in temperature ($22.0 - 17.0 = 5.0$).

Heat (blobs)	Mass of water (g)	Initial T (°C)	Final T (°C)	ΔT (°C)
1	300	17.0	22.0	5.0
2	300			
3	300			
4	300			

From the data you have collected, plot a graph of the change in temperature of the water, ΔT, as a function of the heat added. What do you conclude about the relationship between the amount of heat added to the water and its temperature change?

In the previous experiment, you kept the mass of water constant and varied the amount of heat added to the water. You probably found that the temperature change of the water was proportional to the number of blobs of heat added. What do you think will happen to the temperature change if you keep the amount of heat constant and vary the mass of the water?

To check up on your prediction, you can add one blob of heat, in separate experiments, to 75 g, 150 g, 225 g, and 300 g of cold water. Prepare a data table similar to the following for this series of experiments.

Heat (blobs)	Mass of water (g)	Initial T (°C)	Final T (°C)	ΔT (°C)
1	75			
1	150			
1	225			
1	300			

After you have collected the data, plot a graph of the change in temperature, ΔT, as a function of the mass of water heated. As you can see, the change in temperature decreases as the mass of water increases. This suggests some kind of inverse relationship between these two variables.

Try plotting the temperature change as a function of the inverse of the mass, $(1/m)$. From the graph, how do you know that ΔT is inversely proportional to m, the mass of water heated?

The results from these two experiments probably indicate that the temperature change of the water is proportional to the amount of heat added and inversely proportional to the mass of water heated. These results can be summarized by writing

$$\Delta T \propto H \times \frac{1}{m},$$

where H represents the heat added and $\propto$ is a symbol that means "is proportional to." By finding the constant of proportionality, we can write

$$\Delta T = kH \times \frac{1}{m}, \quad \text{or} \quad \Delta T = k \frac{H}{m}.$$

This expression may also be written as

$$H = Km\,\Delta T, \quad \text{where} \quad K = \frac{1}{k}.$$

This equation tells us that the heat added to the water can be expressed as the product of the mass of the water and its change in temperature multiplied by some constant that makes it equal to the heat measured in blobs.

Here are two ways that you can check up on this relationship.

The first is to use all the data you have collected to plot a graph of the heat, H, added in each trial vs. the product of the mass of the water and its temperature change, $m\Delta T$, for those trials. Is H proportional to $m\Delta T$? If it is, what is the value of the proportionality constant, K?

A second way is to check the relationship experimentally. If $H = Km\Delta T$, then

$$\Delta T = K\frac{H}{m}.$$

This equation tells us that if we keep the ratio of the heat to the mass constant, then the temperature change should also remain constant. You can easily check this by adding one blob of heat to 75 g of cold water, two blobs to 150 g, three blobs to 225 g, and four blobs to 300 g. Does the change in temperature remain very nearly the same in all these trials?

The results of your experiments indicate that while the temperature does increase when heat is added to water, the mass of the water is also involved. Twice as much mass requires twice as much heat to produce the same temperature change.

•   In most laboratories heat is measured in joules or calories, not in blobs. Why? Why can't the blob be used as a universal unit of heat?

•   Some of the chemical energy stored as potential energy in many substances is released when the substances undergo a chemical reaction such as burning. Design an experiment to find out how much energy is released when a gram of candle wax burns. Does the energy stored depend on the kind of candle? **If you decide to do the experiment you've designed, be sure to work under adult supervision.**

•   The *specific heat* of a substance is defined as the amount of heat required to raise or lower the temperature of 1 gram of the substance by 1 degree Celsius (1°C). Design an experiment to find the specific heat of a liquid, such as cooking oil or glycol (antifreeze). Design another experiment to find the specific heat of metals, such as copper and/or steel. **If you decide to do the experiment you've designed, be sure to work under adult supervision.**

THE TEMPERATURE OF A FLAME

The specific heat of steel is approximately 0.11 cal/g/°C. If you drop a hot steel washer into some cold water, the temperature of the water will rise. Heat is transferred from the hot washer to the cold

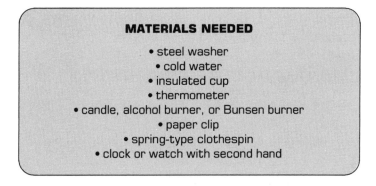

water. Suppose you have 100 g of cold water in an insulated cup. You use forceps to add a hot steel washer, which weighs, say 10 g, to the water. If the temperature of the water rises 5.0°C, you know that 500 calories (100 g × 5.0°C) of heat were transferred to the water. The heat must have come from the hot washer. Because the specific heat of the washer is 0.11 cal/g/°C, it transferred only 0.11 cal per gram per degree drop in its temperature. Since it weighed 10 g, it delivered 10 × 0.11 cal, or 1.1 cal for each degree its temperature fell. The total heat that came from the washer (500 cal) then must be equal to

$$0.11 \text{ cal/g/°C} \times 10g \times \Delta T = 500 \text{ cal.}$$

What was the temperature change of the washer?

Working under adult supervision, use a steel washer, and some cold water in an insulated cup, together with a thermometer, to measure the temperature of a candle flame, an alcohol burner flame, or a Bunsen burner flame. A piece of wire, such as a paper clip, held by a spring-type clothespin can be used to hold the washer in the flame. How can you determine the period of time that the washer should be held in the flame? What is the temperature of the flame according to your experiment?

THE HEAT OF VAPORIZATION

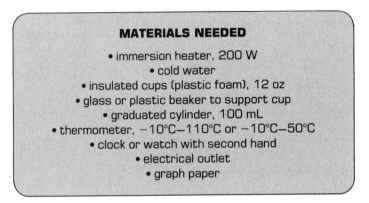

MATERIALS NEEDED
- immersion heater, 200 W
- cold water
- insulated cups (plastic foam), 12 oz
- glass or plastic beaker to support cup
- graduated cylinder, 100 mL
- thermometer, −10°C–110°C or −10°C–50°C
- clock or watch with second hand
- electrical outlet
- graph paper

When water boils, the liquid is converted to a gas—steam. If this is done in an open container at sea level, the temperature remains constant at about 100°C despite the fact that heat is being continuously transferred from the heat source to the water. The energy transferred to the water as heat is the energy required to provide the atomic or molecular potential energy that a gas has by virtue of the fact that its particles are about ten times farther apart than they are in the liquid state.

You can use the immersion heater you used before to heat water to the boiling point and to determine the energy required to change a gram of water from liquid to gas at the boiling point. Place 150 g (150 mL) of cold water in an insulated cup. Put the cup in a glass or plastic beaker to help support the cup. The cup should be large enough so that when the water boils it does not spatter out of the cup.

A coal-fired electric power plant. The steam you see has been used to turn giant turbines that provide our homes with electric energy.

First, find the amount of heat, in calories or joules, that the heater transfers to the water per unit time. This can be done by finding the temperature change of the water when it is heated for 1 minute with the immersion heater. **(Remember, never plug in the heater unless the coil is in water!)**

Next, find out how much water is boiled away when the heater (placed in 150 g of water) operates for a period of 7 or 8 minutes. How much of this heat was used to raise the water to the boiling temperature? How much of the heat was used to change the liquid water to gas? How much heat is required to change 1 gram of water from liquid to gas? (This is called the *heat of vaporization* for water.)

In your calculation, you probably assumed that any heat not used to raise the water temperature to the boiling point was used to vaporize it. But, in fact, some heat is lost to the cooler air that surrounds the boiling water. How can you estimate the heat lost to the cooler surroundings? Once you have figured it out, go back and calculate the heat of vaporization. By how much does your new value differ from the old value?

• When heat is transferred from gaseous water (steam) at the boiling point, the gas condenses to liquid water. How much energy per gram do you think is transferred from the steam during this process? Design an experiment to test your prediction. **Work under adult supervision if you do this experiment, because steam can cause serious burns.**

• Ice melts at a constant temperature called the freezing or melting point (0°C or 32°F). Again, the energy transferred during this change of state is related to the increase (melting) or decrease (freezing) of molecular potential energy. The heat required to melt 1 g of ice at the freezing point is called the *heat of fusion*. Design and carry out an experiment to determine the heat of fusion of ice.

• Design an experiment to show that the elastic potential energy stored in a stretched spring or a lifted mass can be transferred as heat to another body.

• Design an experiment to show that you can transfer heat to a body by doing work.

4

CHALLENGING ELECTRICAL EXPERIMENTS

For the first five years of my life, I lived in a rural home that had no electricity. Modern society has become so dependent on electrical energy that we often fail to realize that it was only during the twentieth century that the use of electrical devices and appliances became widespread. Because electricity is so common today, we should all have a reasonable understanding of what it is and how it works.

A flashlight bulb connected to a battery (D-cell) by one wire, as shown in Figure 24a, will not light. To make the bulb light, you can touch the base of the bulb to the other pole of the battery, as shown in Figure 24b, or run a second wire from the base of the bulb to the other battery terminal.

If a generator is used in place of the battery, the bulb must be connected to both of its poles. Any household appliance or battery-operated instrument has two contacts that must be connected to make the device work. The fact that all electrical devices must be connected to both poles of a battery or generator gave rise to a model of electricity that is used to explain electric circuits. According to the model, electric charges "flow" from one pole of a battery or generator, through

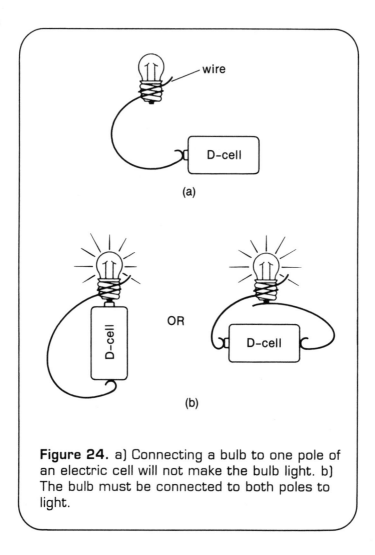

Figure 24. a) Connecting a bulb to one pole of an electric cell will not make the bulb light. b) The bulb must be connected to both poles to light.

the electrical device, and back to the other pole of the electrical source. There will be no flow of charge unless the device is connected to both poles and unless the charges have energy. That energy comes from the chemical energy stored in the battery or the work done on the generator.

MEASURING ELECTRIC CHARGE

MATERIALS NEEDED

- two ammeters, 0– to 1.0–A range
- two or three D-cells or variable low voltage d.c. power source
- connecting wires
- flashlight bulbs
- voltmeter, 0–3 or 0–15 V

Electric charge can be measured with an ammeter *and* a clock. If you examine an ammeter, you will see that the units on the meter are amperes (A). Since the needle on an ammeter remains steady when it is placed in a circuit, such as the one shown in Figure 25*a*, it must measure the *rate* of charge flow (electric current), not charge. If it measured charge, the needle would move slowly across the dial as more charge moved along the circuit. Since an ampere measures charge per time, we can measure charge as the product of current, in amperes, and time, in seconds. Thus,

$$\text{Charge} = \text{current} \times \text{time}, \quad \text{or} \quad \text{Charge} = \frac{\text{charge}}{\text{time}} \times \text{time}.$$

For example, suppose a current of 0.70 A flows for 60 s. The charge that flows, in ampere-seconds (A-S), is given by

$$0.70 \text{ A} \times 60 \text{ s} = 42 \text{ A-s}.$$

Ideally, scientific instruments should have no effect on what they measure. A ruler, for example, does not change the length of the object being measured. A thermometer, however, may alter the temperature of a liquid in which it is placed,

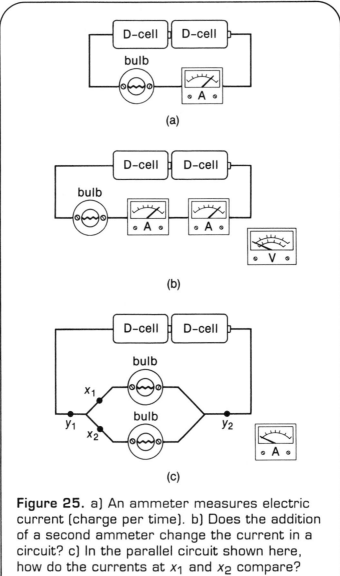

(a)

(b)

(c)

Figure 25. a) An ammeter measures electric current (charge per time). b) Does the addition of a second ammeter change the current in a circuit? c) In the parallel circuit shown here, how do the currents at x_1 and x_2 compare? How do the currents at y_1 and y_2 compare? How does the sum of the currents at x_1 and x_2 compare with the current at y_1 and y_2?

particularly if the volume of the liquid is small and it is much colder or hotter than the thermometer. To see what effect an ammeter has on the current it measures, set up the circuit shown in Figure 25a, which consists of two D-cells, connecting wires, and a flashlight bulb. If the current through the bulb is too small to measure accurately, add another D-cell to your battery or use a variable-voltage d.c. power source. If you use a power source, start at zero and increase the voltage in small increments to prevent burning out the bulb. If you use D-cells, don't let the circuit operate for very long; it could wear down the D-cells quite rapidly.

What does the ammeter tell you about the current through the bulb? What must be the current through the ammeter? Substitute a second, similar ammeter for the first one. How closely do the meter readings agree? Now connect the two ammeters in series as shown in Figure 25b. Does an ammeter significantly change the current it is designed to measure?

Now replace one of the ammeters with a voltmeter. Does a voltmeter have any effect on the current? Do you think a voltmeter can be used to measure current?

Using two bulbs and several D-cells or a variable-voltage d.c. power source, set up the parallel circuit shown in Figure 25c. Use an ammeter to find the current through each bulb by inserting the ammeter (or two identical ammeters, if you have them) at points x_1 and x_2. Try to predict what the ammeters will read when placed at points y_1 and y_2 in the circuit. Were you right?

WHAT DOES A VOLTMETER MEASURE?

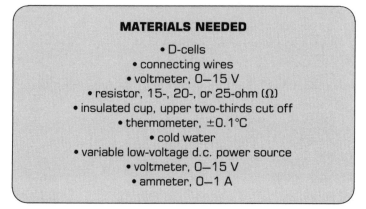

MATERIALS NEEDED

- D-cells
- connecting wires
- voltmeter, 0–15 V
- resistor, 15-, 20-, or 25-ohm (Ω)
- insulated cup, upper two-thirds cut off
- thermometer, ±0.1°C
- cold water
- variable low-voltage d.c. power source
- voltmeter, 0–15 V
- ammeter, 0–1 A

One thing a voltmeter can measure is the number of D-cells connected in series (end to end). To see this for yourself, use wires to connect a voltmeter to first one, then two, then three, then . . . D-cells in series as shown in Figure 26. Plot a graph of the voltmeter reading as a function of the number of D-cells in series. What is the voltage across one cell? How can you use a voltmeter to count D-cells?

You've probably heard that a voltmeter measures voltage or potential difference. But what does that mean? To find out, connect a voltmeter with a 0- to 15-volt scale in parallel with an electric heater (resistor) and ammeter as shown in Figure 27.

A 15-, 20-, or 25-ohm resistor can serve as the heater. Since the resistor may operate beyond its recommended power, it should be connected only when in water. Submerge it in 50 g of cold water in an insulated cup that has had its upper two-thirds cut off as shown. Use the thermometer to

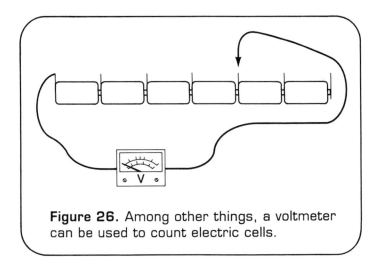

Figure 26. Among other things, a voltmeter can be used to count electric cells.

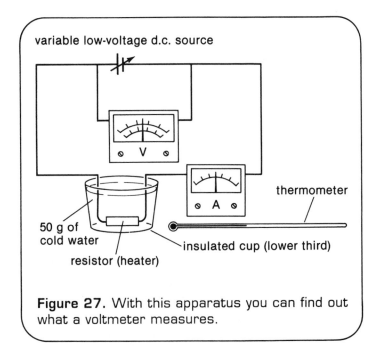

variable low-voltage d.c. source

thermometer

50 g of cold water

insulated cup (lower third)

resistor (heater)

Figure 27. With this apparatus you can find out what a voltmeter measures.

measure the temperature of the water, which should be about 2°C–3°C below room temperature. This will compensate for heat losses when the water temperature rises above that of the room.

Record the temperature of the cool water in the insulated cup to the nearest 0.10°C, if possible. Set the variable-voltage d.c. source so that a current of approximately 0.80 A flows through the heater immersed in water for a period of 90 seconds. Record the voltmeter and ammeter readings as the current flows. After the run is completed, stir the water thoroughly and record its final temperature.

What was the change in temperature of the water? How much heat, in calories, was produced by the electric current?

In succeeding runs, starting with fresh cool water each time, let a current of 0.70 A flow for 2 minutes (120 s), then 0.60 A for 2.5 minutes, then 0.50 A for 3.5 minutes, and, finally, 0.30 A for 5 minutes. Record the voltage, current, time, and temperature changes of the water for each run. What is the source of the heat transferred to the water?

When you have collected all the data, calculate the heat transferred to the water, in calories, and the charge that flowed, in ampere-seconds, for each run. Plot a graph of *heat per charge*, in cal/A-s, on the vertical axis vs. the voltmeter readings, in volts, on the horizontal axis. What does the graph tell you? What does a voltmeter measure?

Use the graph to write an equation relating heat per charge and voltage. Since charge is cur-

One of the largest currents you'll ever
see occurs when lightning flashes.

rent × time, write an equation relating heat, current, time, and voltage.

The product of voltage × current × time is called *electric work* or *electric energy*; it is measured in units called joules (J). It is an example of how one form of energy, in this case electrical energy, can be converted to heat. Because the heat came from the electrical work, the heat transferred can be measured in joules just as well as calories. If you measure the heat transferred in joules, what is the equation that relates heat, current, time, and voltage? How many joules are equal to 1 calorie, according to your measurements? What is a volt in terms of joules and ampere-seconds?

• In the previous experiment, you probably found that the heat transferred by an electric current is related to the voltage, current, and time by the following equation:

$$\text{Heat} = \text{voltage} \times \text{current} \times \text{time} \quad \text{or} \quad H = VIt,$$

where heat, H, is measured in joules; voltage, V, in volts, current, I, in amperes, and time, t, in seconds.

According to this relationship, if the voltage remains constant, the heat transferred should be proportional to the charge that flows in the circuit. Design and carry out an experiment to test this deduction.

• Connect two D-cells in parallel (side by side, not end to end). What do you think the voltmeter reading across these cells will be? Could a voltmeter be used to measure the number of D-cells in parallel?

SIMPLE ELECTRIC CIRCUITS

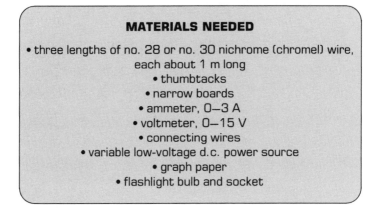

MATERIALS NEEDED

- three lengths of no. 28 or no. 30 nichrome (chromel) wire, each about 1 m long
- thumbtacks
- narrow boards
- ammeter, 0—3 A
- voltmeter, 0—15 V
- connecting wires
- variable low-voltage d.c. power source
- graph paper
- flashlight bulb and socket

Obtain two pieces of no. 28 or no. 30 nichrome (chromel) wire, each about 1 m long. Use thumbtacks to fasten the wires to two narrow boards, each about 1 m long, as shown in Figure 28. Then connect the ends of one wire to an ammeter, voltmeter, and variable-voltage d.c. power source as shown. Be sure the meters are properly connected with regard to sign (+ or −).

To prevent overheating, turn on the power source only long enough to make meter readings.

Vary the length of nichrome wire connected to the power source until the ammeter reads about 1 A when the voltmeter reads about 10 V. Move the thumbtacks to mark the ends of this length of wire. You may want to cut off any excess wire. Do the same thing with the other wire. With this apparatus, you can carry out a number of investigations.

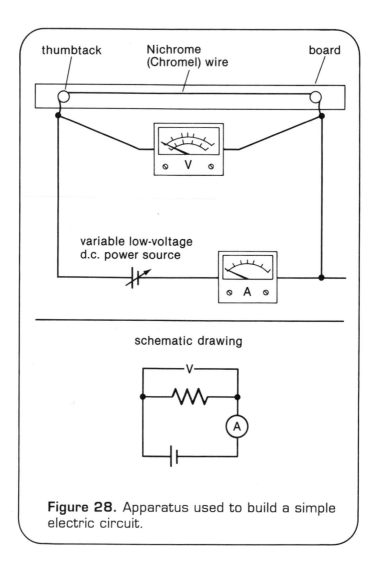

Figure 28. Apparatus used to build a simple electric circuit.

Investigation 1: How Is the Current through a Wire Related to the Voltage (Potential Difference) across the Wire?

Use the variable-voltage d.c. power source to change the voltage across the wire from 3 to 6, to

9, to 12 volts. Record the current for each voltage. Remember, **turn on the power source only long enough to make meter readings.** Record the voltmeter and ammeter readings for each trial you make. Then plot a graph of current, in amperes, vs. the voltage, or potential difference, in volts. What can you conclude from the graph? Write the equation given by your graph. This relationship is known as *Ohm's law.*

The ratio of the voltage to the current for any given wire is defined as the resistance of the wire. What is the resistance of the wire you are using? Resistance is measured in units called ohms, in honor of Georg Ohm. One volt per ampere is a resistance of 1 ohm. What is the resistance of your wire in ohms?

Investigation 2: How Does the Resistance of a Wire Vary with Its Length?

Design and conduct an experiment to answer this question. What do you find?

Investigation 3: How Is the Resistance of a Wire Affected by Temperature?

You were cautioned earlier to turn on the power source only long enough to read the meters. To see why, keep the voltage across the wire constant and watch the ammeter. Hold your hand close to, but not touching, the wire. What happens to the temperature of the wire as current continues to flow through it? What happens to the current as the temperature of the wire changes? How is the resistance of the wire affected by increasing temperatures?

Use the data in Table 3 to establish a specific quantitative relationship between resistance and temperature. Plot the resistance of the wire as a function of the temperature. What do you find?

Table 3: The Resistance of a 1000-Meter Length of No. 14 Copper Wire at Different Temperatures

Temperature (°C)	Resistance (Ω)
0	7.635
20	8.284
50	9.262
75	10.075

Investigation 4: What Is the Resistance of a Flashlight Bulb?

Design an experiment to measure the resistance of the filament of a flashlight bulb. **(Be careful not to exceed its voltage limits or you may melt the bulb's filament.)** Is the resistance of the bulb's filament constant, or does it vary with the current? How can you explain your results?

Investigation 5: How Does the Resistance of a Wire Vary with Its Area of Cross Section?

You can use the data in Table 4 to plot a graph of resistance as a function of cross-sectional area. Plot the data for both kinds of wire on the same graph. According to the graphs you've made, how is the resistance of a wire related to its cross-sectional area? Which of the two metals is a better conductor of electricity?

Table 4: The Resistance of Copper and Aluminum Wires with Different Cross-Sectional Areas*

For copper wire		For aluminum wire	
Cross section (cm²)	Resistance (Ω)	Cross section (cm²)	Resistance (Ω)
0.033	5.210	0.033	8.563
0.066	2.599	0.066	4.265
0.133	1.296	0.133	2.126
0.266	0.646	0.266	1.060
0.535	0.322	0.535	0.528

*All wires were 1000 m long, and the resistance was measured at 20°C.

Investigation 6: Does an Electroplating Cell Follow Ohm's Law?

You've seen that the electrical resistance of a wire depends on its length, cross-sectional area, temperature, and composition. What variables affect the resistance of an electroplating cell, such as the copper plating cell shown in Figure 29? Does such a cell follow Ohm's law?

To build such a cell, you'll need a 1-molar solution of copper sulfate, which you can prepare by dissolving 250 g of copper sulfate crystals ($CuSO_4 \cdot 5H_2O$) in enough water to make 1 liter of solution. **Put on safety goggles before you pour** about 200 mL of the blue solution into a 250-mL beaker. Fasten clean sheet copper or copper mesh electrodes, 5 cm × 10 cm (2 in × 4 in) to opposite sides of the beaker. Connect a variable-voltage d.c. power source to the cell after connecting an ammeter in series with the cell and a voltmeter in parallel.

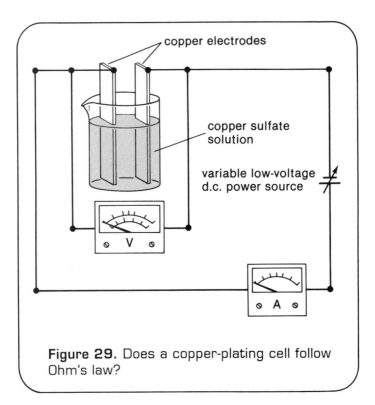

Figure 29. Does a copper-plating cell follow Ohm's law?

Vary the voltage across the cell and read the ammeter for each voltage you establish. Plot a graph of current as a function of voltage. Does the copper plating cell follow Ohm's law?

Design experiments to answer the following questions:

•   Is the resistance of a copper plating cell affected by the temperature of the solution?

•   Does the temperature of the solution change significantly when an electric current flows through it? If it does, what can you do to prevent temperature changes during your experiments?

•   Is the resistance of the cell affected by the distance between the two copper electrodes? Is it affected by the area of the electrodes in contact with the solution?

•   Is the resistance of the cell affected by the concentration of the copper sulfate solution?

•   If you've studied chemistry, how can you determine the number of moles of copper that dissolve and plate out when a current of approximately 1.0 A flows for 20 minutes? How does the number of moles of copper that dissolve or plate compare with the number of moles of electrons that flow during the electroplating? Hint: an ampere constitutes a charge flow of 6.24×10^{18} electrons per second.

Investigation 7: What Is the Resistance of Two Resistors Wired in Series?

Determine the resistance of the second piece of nichrome wire (R_2) you fastened to a board. Then connect the two wires (R_1 and R_2) in series (one after the other) as shown in Figure 30. Insert the ammeter between the resistors (point x in the diagram) and establish a voltage of about 10 to 12 V across the entire circuit. What is the resistance of the two wires in series? If you keep the voltage fixed, what do you think the ammeter will read if you connect it into the circuit at position x'? At position x"? Were you right? How does the current through resistor R_1 compare with the current through resistor R_2? Would you be surprised if the current through both resistors were not the same?

What do you think a second voltmeter will read if it is connected across R_1? Across R_2? Were you right?

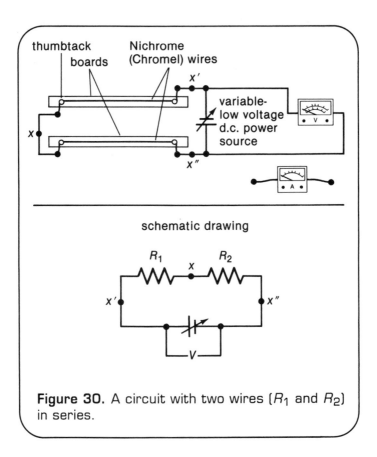

Figure 30. A circuit with two wires (R_1 and R_2) in series.

From the results of your investigation, what would be the total resistance in a circuit that consisted of two resistors, R_1 and R_2, connected in series? If the voltage across R_1 were V_1 and the voltage across R_2 were V_2, what would be the voltage across the entire circuit?

What do you think the total resistance across three resistors, R_1, R_2, and R_3, would be? Carry out an experiment to test your prediction.

Investigation 8: What Is the Resistance of Two Resistors Wired in Parallel?

Build the circuit shown in Figure 31 using the two resistors you used in Investigation 7. This time the resistors are connected in parallel (side by side). Given the circuit, why is the voltage across each resistor the same? How do you think arranging the wires in this manner will affect their total resistance? Hint: In Table 4, what happens to the resistance when the cross-sectional area doubles?

If you establish a voltage of about 10 V across the entire circuit, what reading do you expect to find on the ammeter if it is inserted at x? At x'? Were you right?

What current would you expect to find in R_1? In R_2? Keeping the voltage fixed, place the ammeter at positions x_1 and then at x_2 to see whether your predictions are correct. Will the current readings you found at x_1 and x_2 be different if you place the ammeter at x_1' and x_2'?

What single resistor, used in place of the two in parallel, would result in the same total current flow through the circuit? Such a resistor is called an *equivalent* resistor.

One way to understand parallel resistors is to use a traffic analogy. When one highway divides into two roads and the speeds of the cars remain constant, the *sum* of the number of vehicles per minute moving along the two roads must equal the number per minute moving along the single highway. If the cars correspond to charges and the roads to wires, you can see that if the conductivity along a single wire is K and the conduc-

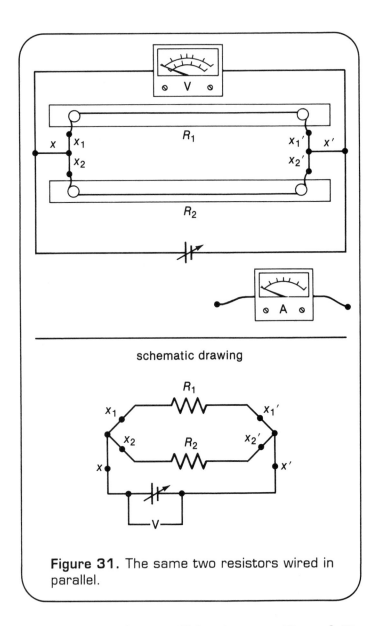

Figure 31. The same two resistors wired in parallel.

tivities along the parallel wires are K_1 and K_2, then $K = K_1 + K_2$. Since conductivity is the inverse of resistance, we may write

$$\frac{1}{R} = \frac{1}{R_1} + \frac{1}{R_2}.$$

The equivalent resistance of R_1 and R_2 in parallel then is R. Does this relationship work for the resistors you used?

What would be the equivalent resistance of three 10-ohm resistors wired in parallel?

PREDICTIONS USING A FLASHLIGHT BULB CIRCUIT

Set up the circuit shown in Figure 32. The bulbs, a, b, and c, are flashlight bulbs in sockets. If possible, use a GE no. 13 bulb for a and GE no. 41 bulbs for b and c.

Connect the voltmeter across the entire circuit (P_1 to P_3) and use the variable low-voltage d.c. power source to establish a potential difference of 5 to 6 V. Maintain this voltage throughout the experiment, but **turn off the power when making new connections.** Record all your data.

Use the ammeter to measure the current at P_1. Then predict the current at P_3. Move the ammeter to that position and test your prediction. Were you right?

Connect the ammeter so that you can measure the current through bulb a. Predict the current through bulb b. Then measure the current through bulb b. Were you right?

Measure the voltage from P_1 to P_2, across the two bulbs wired in parallel. Then predict the voltage across bulb c (P_2 to P_3). Measure the voltage across bulb c. Was your prediction correct?

From the data you have collected, determine the resistances of bulbs a, b, and c. Determine the

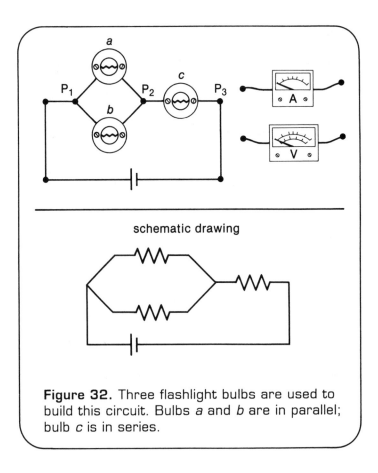

Figure 32. Three flashlight bulbs are used to build this circuit. Bulbs *a* and *b* are in parallel; bulb *c* is in series.

equivalent resistance of the two bulbs wired in parallel. Use a length of the nichrome wire you used in the previous series of investigations to build a resistor equivalent to the two bulbs in parallel. How can you show that this piece of wire is the equivalent of the two bulbs in parallel? In what way does this equivalent resistor differ from the two bulbs in parallel?

The power, in watts (W), developed in a bulb, that is, the energy per time, can be determined

Power companies read meters like this one before they send a bill to the owner. The numbers on the dial indicate kilowatt hours, which is a measure of electrical energy.

from the product of the current and the voltage. After all, voltage is measured in volts or joules per ampere-second (J/A-s) and current is measured in amperes. The product of these two quantities, therefore, is J/s, or watts:

$$\frac{J}{A\text{-}s} \times A = \frac{J}{s} \quad \text{or} \quad W.$$

How much power was developed in bulb a? Bulb b? Bulb c? How much power was developed across the entire circuit? How much electrical energy would be produced in the circuit in 1 minute? In what two forms would that energy appear? Which form do you think would predominate? Design and conduct an experiment to test your prediction.

If your measurements were accurate, you probably found that the resistances of bulbs b and c were different even though the bulbs are supposed to be identical. Is this because the bulbs are really different?

To find out, loosen bulb a so that bulbs b and c, which are identical, are in series. Measure the voltage across each one. Are their resistances very nearly the same? How can the same bulb have two resistances depending on its position in the circuit shown in Figure 32? Hint: remember what you learned in Investigation 3 of the previous series of experiments.

• On all electrical appliances you will find a power rating. Since most electrical appliances are connected to 120-V circuits (some appliances, such as water heaters, clothes dryers, and kitchen ranges, are connected to 240-V circuits), it's easy to figure out how much current flows in each appliance. For example, suppose you have a 1200-W toaster. Since power (P) equals the product of current (I) and voltage (V), the current can be calculated easily.

$$P = V \times I \text{ therefore, } I = \frac{P}{V} = \frac{1200 \text{ J/s}}{120 \text{ J/A-s}} = 10 \text{ A.}$$

Knowing the current through the toaster and the voltage across it, you can easily calculate the resistance of the toaster wire to be 12 Ω.

Calculate the current you can expect to find in a 100-W light bulb when it is operating in a 120-V circuit. What is the resistance of the filament in such a bulb? **Don't attempt to measure the currents and voltages of household electric circuits!**

A HIGH-VOLTAGE BULB
IN A LOW-VOLTAGE CIRCUIT

Disconnect a lamp with a 100-W light bulb from its electrical outlet. Connect its leads instead to a low-voltage d.c. power source as shown in Figure 33. Use the power source to increase the voltage across the bulb to about 15 V. Then read the ammeter to find the current through the bulb. What is the resistance of the bulb's filament on the basis of these measurements? How does it compare with the resistance that you calculated in the preceding section? How can you explain the difference in the filament's resistance under these different conditions?

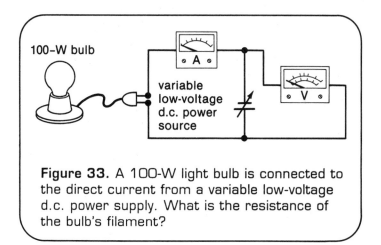

Figure 33. A 100-W light bulb is connected to the direct current from a variable low-voltage d.c. power supply. What is the resistance of the bulb's filament?

5

CHALLENGING EXPERIMENTS IN BIOLOGY

My first teaching assignment was in biology, which was also my major in college. I enjoyed teaching the subject, and many students were as fascinated with biology as I was. However, I found it difficult to use the subject matter to convey a sense of what scientific inquiry is all about. Biology is so complex, there are so many variables, and so much of it depends on an understanding of chemistry and physics that I found it extremely difficult to teach in the way I think science should be taught. A teacher who is satisfied to have students memorize terms may be quite comfortable teaching biology as an exercise in memory, but I always wanted students to understand the science involved, to know *how* we know. If I had been able to teach biology to students who were already familiar with chemistry and physics, I would have felt much more comfortable as a biology teacher.

In this chapter I've tried to choose challenging biology experiments that are interesting to do and require a minimum of physics and chemistry. But, as you'll see, it's very difficult to exclude these subjects entirely.

PLANTS, LIGHT, AND AIR

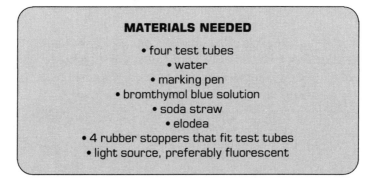

MATERIALS NEEDED

- four test tubes
- water
- marking pen
- bromthymol blue solution
- soda straw
- elodea
- 4 rubber stoppers that fit test tubes
- light source, preferably fluorescent

Scientists are concerned about the growing concentration of carbon dioxide (CO_2) in the atmosphere because it may bring about an increase in global temperatures. The problem is compounded by the destruction of tropical rain forests to make grazing land for cattle. One way to combat this effect is to grow more trees, not fewer, because the cells in leaves carry on photosynthesis. During photosynthesis, carbon dioxide is chemically joined with water in the presence of chlorophyll and sunlight to form food (sugar and starch) and release oxygen, the gas essential for respiration. In this experiment, you'll have an opportunity to observe the interaction of a plant and carbon dioxide under different conditions.

Half-fill four test tubes with water. Use a marking pen to number the tubes 1, 2, 3, and 4. Add 1 mL of bromthymol blue solution to each of the tubes. Bromthymol blue is an acid-base indicator that turns yellow in an acid and blue in a base. It becomes yellow in the presence of a carbon dioxide solution because carbon dioxide reacts with water to form a weak acid, H_2CO_3 (carbonic acid).

Why does this plant bend toward the window?

Use a soda straw to blow gently into tubes 1 and 2. What color change occurs? How can you account for the yellow color of the indicator?

Put a sprig of elodea (a water plant) in tubes 1 and 3. Then seal all four tubes with rubber stoppers and put them near a bright light. (The tubes should not be so close that they get hot.) After several hours, observe the tubes. Observe them again after several more hours. What changes can you observe? How can you explain your observations? What is the purpose of each tube in this experiment?

What do you think will happen in each tube if you repeat the experiment but keep the tubes in darkness? Test your predictions by doing the experiment again, this time in darkness. Were your predictions correct?

HOLES IN LEAVES

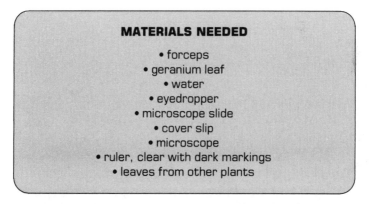

MATERIALS NEEDED

- forceps
- geranium leaf
- water
- eyedropper
- microscope slide
- cover slip
- microscope
- ruler, clear with dark markings
- leaves from other plants

I developed this experiment many years ago in an effort to include more mathematics in biology. Far too often biology is taught with a minimum of mathematics, a practice that fails to make students aware of the important role of mathematics in science.

This experiment uses the underside of a leaf to develop a need for mathematics. A close look at a leaf's "skin" reveals many openings (stomates) that allow gases to enter and leave the cells within the leaf. These openings are bordered by bean-shaped cells, appropriately called guard cells, that control the size of the openings.

To see some stomates, fold a geranium leaf and use forceps to peel away a small section of the leaf's lower epidermis. Mount the tissue in a drop of water on a microscope slide, cover with a glass cover slip, and examine the tissue under a microscope. Once you can identify the stomates, examine other sections of the same leaf tissue under the microscope. For each section, count the number of stomates that you see using the low-power lens. What is the average number of stomates that you observe?

How can you determine the area that you see through the low-power lens? Once you have determined the visible area, calculate the stomate density of a geranium leaf, that is, the number of stomates per unit area. Estimate the total number of stomates on a geranium leaf and on the entire plant.

Examine leaves from other plants. Do these plants have stomates on the surface of their leaves? Does stomate density seem to be relatively constant from plant to plant, or does it differ significantly with the species of plant?

• How do you think the guard cells control the movement of gases, especially water vapor, in and out of the leaves? Design and carry out an experiment to test your idea.

MAKING PLANTS BEND

MATERIALS NEEDED

- growing plant
- window that admits lots of sunlight
- soil and pot
- vermiculite or soil
- water
- corn, bean, or radish seeds
- clear plastic containers
- corn seed
- old record turntable
- variety of seeds: bean, radish, oat, corn, grass, different flowers, etc.
- pie plates

People like to watch plants change with time. It's interesting to watch seeds germinate, grow, flower, and produce fruit and new seeds. It's even more interesting if you have some questions that can be answered by watching the plants and controlling the conditions where they germinate and grow. I'll ask a few to get you started. After you've done experiments to answer these questions, you'll probably have many more that you can pursue on your own.

To begin, place a growing plant near a window and leave it there for a few days. Be sure to keep the soil in which the plant is growing moist, but not wet. Does the plant bend toward the light? If it does, what happens when you turn the plant around? Does its direction of growth change? Can you make it grow in a corkscrew pattern?

Choose a plant that grows toward light. Design an experiment to find out whether the plant is more attracted to one color of light than to another. How can you be sure that the plant is responding to differences in color and not to differences in the intensity of the light?

Plant some corn, bean, or radish seeds in vermiculite or soil in clear plastic containers so you can watch the seeds as they germinate. In which direction do the roots grow? How about the stems? Once the seeds have germinated, turn the box on its side. What happens to the growth direction of the roots and stems now?

Can you use light to make stems grow down toward the Earth? Can you make roots grow up toward the sky?

Fasten a pie plate of corn seedlings growing in soil or vermiculite to an old record turntable. Leave the seedlings on the turntable as it rotates for several days. Leave an identical container of corn seedlings, as a control experiment, on a nearby stationary pie plate. How do the growth patterns of the two sets of seedlings compare? How can you explain the differences? What happens to the growth pattern of the seedlings on the turntable after they stop rotating?

How do you think the growth pattern of the seedlings will be affected by increasing or decreasing the rotation rate of the turntable? Test your hypothesis in a separate experiment. Were you right?

How do you think seeds would grow under conditions of weightlessness such as one finds in a spaceship? How could an artificial gravity be created in such a spaceship?

• Obtain a variety of seeds—bean, radish, oat, corn, grass, different flowers, etc. Design an experiment to see whether storing these seeds at different temperatures has any effect on their germination rate, that is, the percentage of the seeds that will germinate after being stored for some period of time.

A CRICKET THERMOMETER

MATERIALS NEEDED

• crickets
• thermometer
• large jar
• nylon stocking or cloth gauze
• rubber band

Some people claim you can use a cricket as a thermometer. They say that if you count the number of times a cricket chirps in 15 seconds and then add 40, you will get a number equal to the temperature in degrees Fahrenheit. Others claim that you should add 50 to the number of cricket chirps to obtain the temperature.

Listen for a cricket. When you find one, check up on each of these two rules. Does either one seem to work reasonably well (within a few degrees)? If it does, how would you modify the rule in order to obtain the temperature in degrees Celsius?

To see whether the rule works for a range of temperatures, capture or buy (from a bait store) a chirping cricket and put it in a large transparent jar along with a thermometer. Cover the mouth of the jar with a nylon stocking or a piece of cloth gauze. Hold the cover in place with a rubber band just below the mouth of the jar. Put the jar in a cool place such as a basement. When the cricket's chirping rate becomes constant again, use the rule to calculate the temperature. Then look at the thermometer. How closely do the actual and calculated temperatures agree?

Next place the jar in a warm place such as an attic on a warm day. Again, compare the calculated and actual temperatures once the cricket's chirping rate becomes constant. Does either rule seem to work reasonably well? If so, over what temperature range is it accurate to within a few degrees?

A LIGHT IN THE DARKNESS

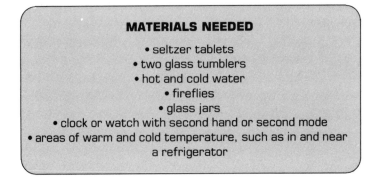

MATERIALS NEEDED

- seltzer tablets
- two glass tumblers
- hot and cold water
- fireflies
- glass jars
- clock or watch with second hand or second mode
- areas of warm and cold temperature, such as in and near a refrigerator

The darkness of a warm spring or summer night is often interrupted by the flashing lights of fireflies. The light is produced by a chemical reaction involving oxygen and a chemical called luciferin. The cold light emitted by the reaction, which is called bioluminescence, is similar to that emitted by the light sticks used by boaters. When these flexible light sticks are bent, a vial is broken, releasing a chemical that reacts with another substance in the stick to produce a greenish light that will last for hours.

Many chemical reactions are affected by temperature. You can see that this is true by dropping a seltzer tablet into a glass of cold water. At the same time drop a second identical tablet into a glass of hot water. How does temperature affect the rate at which seltzer reacts with water?

Will temperature have a similar effect on the rate at which fireflies produce light? To find out, you'll have to capture a couple of fireflies. Put each one in a separate glass jar. Measure the rate at which the fireflies produce light. Do they all produce light at about the same rate? If not, label each jar and measure and record the flashing rate for each fly.

Place the jars on top and near the back of a refrigerator where it is warm. Allow a few minutes for the flies to adjust to the higher temperature, then measure the flashing rate of the flies again. Has it changed?

Now put the jars inside the refrigerator. After a few minutes, again measure the flashing rate. Do your results suggest that the rate at which fireflies produce flashes of light is related to the temperature of their surroundings? If it is, can you find a mathematical relationship between the flashing rate and the temperature?

• Design an experiment to see whether the concentration of oxygen affects the firefly's flashing rate. Then, **under the supervision and guidance of a science teacher,** carry out your experiment. What do you find?

SPIDERS AND THEIR WEBS

MATERIALS NEEDED

- gloves
- small stick
- glass jar
- nails, hammer, ruler, and saw
- soil, twigs, and dead leaves
- paper towel or cotton
- plastic vial
- rubbing alcohol
- magnifying glass
- garden spider
- 1-in × 2-in boards, 10 ft long
- large shallow pan
- spray can of light-colored paint
- dark paper

David Webster, a close friend now deceased, with whom I coauthored several books, once wrote a book about spiders. I had never realized how fascinating these creatures were until I read his book, *Spider Watching.* Most spiders are harmless; however, the bite of a few such as the black widow and brown recluse spider can be serious. To be on the safe side, **wear gloves and move spiders with a small stick.**

Spiders can usually be found indoors in basements or garages, or outdoors under windowsills or on foundations. They can also be found under stones or logs or in flowers and tall grass. Of course, fresh webs indicate that a spider cannot be far away.

If you find a spider, use a stick to push the spider into a glass jar. Before you capture the spider, remove the jar's lid and punch some holes in it so air can enter and leave the container. The spider cannot easily climb the jar's smooth walls. Add some soil, twigs, and a few dead leaves to the bottom of the jar. A wad of wet paper towel or cotton will provide water for the spider. Watch the spider for a few days. Does it spin a web? What does it like to eat? What does the spider do when you turn it loose? If you catch a spider with an egg sac, you may see the eggs hatch and find many more, little spiders inside the jar.

You can prepare a collection of spiders for close examination. Drop a spider into a clear plastic vial that contains rubbing alcohol and put the cover back on. The alcohol will kill and preserve them. Using a magnifying glass and a library reference book, you may be able to identify the various parts of the animals as well as the species of spiders that you have captured and preserved.

Spider Webs

Some, but not all, spiders spin webs. Some webs are flimsy and short-lived, such as the thin filmy webs you find spun on dew-covered grass. Orb webs, like the one shown in Figure 34, are the most beautiful webs spun by spiders. Webs you ordinarily might not see are often made visible by the morning sunlight reflected from dewdrops clinging to the fine filaments. Although these webs are often spun at night, you may be able to watch an orb-weaving spider make a web. Despite such a web's beautiful design, a spider can prepare one in less than an hour. Since spiders don't

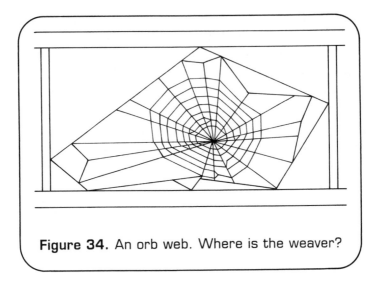

Figure 34. An orb web. Where is the weaver?

fly, how does the spider connect the web from one leaf, branch, stick, or board to another? You'll find a gentle breeze helps the orb weaver accomplish its difficult task.

Once you find a freshly spun orb web, can you find the spider who wove it? Perhaps you can entice the spider to reveal its presence by gently jiggling the web with a pencil. Watch to see what happens on the web's surface. Do the filaments dry out? Does the spider ever repair the web? What happens when an insect becomes trapped in the web? How does the spider react?

Another way to watch an orb web is to have a spider build one for you. The garden spider, which is orange and black, lives in tall grass and weeds. With some careful searching, you can probably find one and capture it in a glass jar. Once you have the spider, build a small wooden frame about a foot on each side from 1 in × 2 in boards. Mount the frame on a pair of similar boards about 2 ft long. Nail 6-in-long feet to these two boards so that the boards and the frame they support can stand upright. Now place the whole structure upright in a large (about 18 in × 12 in), shallow pan of water. Because garden spiders can't swim, the water will cause the spider to stay on the frame once you put it there. Be sure you keep water in the pan; otherwise the spider will walk away.

After several days the spider will probably adjust to its new surroundings and spin a web. If you occasionally throw a few flies or other small insects onto the web, the spider will live there for many weeks and you'll be able to observe its behavior.

When you've learned all you want from your spider, remove the wooden frame from the water. Does the spider continue to live on the frame, or does it now escape from captivity into the high grass that was its former home?

Preserving Webs

You can preserve a spider web by spraying it with a light-colored paint and then holding a sheet of dark paper against it. Be sure the web is dry and free of dewdrops. Hold a can of spray paint about 50–70 cm from one side of the web. Spray the web lightly, starting from the center and working your way outward around the web. Repeat the process from the other side of the web. While the paint is still wet, press the paper gently against the web. Cut away the threads that support the web at its edges and gently lift away the web on the paper.

After the paint has dried, you can cover the paper with clear plastic wrap. You could use this technique to preserve and frame a variety of webs made by different spiders.

ANIMAL BEHAVIOR

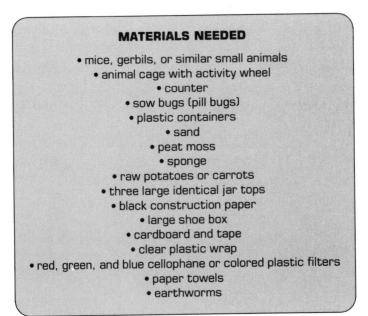

MATERIALS NEEDED

• mice, gerbils, or similar small animals
• animal cage with activity wheel
• counter
• sow bugs (pill bugs)
• plastic containers
• sand
• peat moss
• sponge
• raw potatoes or carrots
• three large identical jar tops
• black construction paper
• large shoe box
• cardboard and tape
• clear plastic wrap
• red, green, and blue cellophane or colored plastic filters
• paper towels
• earthworms

If you own a pet, you probably know a lot about animal behavior already even though you haven't studied it in a scientific manner. In this experiment, you'll investigate some aspects of the behavior of three different animals. Of course, you can choose which, if any, of the animals you want to investigate.

Mice, Gerbils, or Similar Animals

If you have pet mice, you can learn a lot about how their activity levels are related to the time of day by placing an activity wheel in their cage. Figure out a way to connect a hand counter to the cage so that it can be used to count the number of times the cage turns.

Now that you have a way of recording the cage turns, find out how many times the cage turns between 6:00 A.M. and 6:00 P.M.; between 6:00 P.M. and 6:00 A.M. Do your mice seem to be more active at night or during the day? Figure out a way to determine at which hours the mice are most active and least active. How do the times of their maximum and minimum activity compare with yours?

Investigate the activity of individual mice. Are all mice active at about the same times of the day? Are some mice much more active than others? Is their activity related to their age? Their sex? Their weight?

How can you use the diameter of the activity wheel and the number of turns to figure out how far an animal runs in one day? What is the average distance traveled per day?

Suppose you keep the light on all the time in the room where the mice live. How does it affect their periods of maximum and minimum activity? Suppose you keep the mice in darkness all the time (except when you feed and water them or clean their cages). How does darkness affect their periods of maximum and minimum activity?

Sow Bugs

You probably wouldn't keep sow bugs as pets, but you can carry out some interesting investigations of their behavior. You can find sow bugs, sometimes called pill bugs or wood lice, in damp places such as under stones, logs, and leaves, where they feed on decaying vegetation.

You can keep the sow bugs you find in a plastic container that has some sand mixed with peat moss. Because they require moisture, you should keep a moist sponge in the container. Add a piece of raw potato or carrot from time to time.

Once your sow bug culture is established, cover the bottom of a deep container with sand. Put three large identical jar tops in the container so that their open tops are level with the sand. Put some dry peat moss in one jar top, moist peat moss in a second, and wet peat moss in the third. Cover half of each jar top with black construction paper so that the bugs can choose between light and dark as well as dry, moist, or wet peat moss. Put the container under a bright light and add about twenty sow bugs to the environment you have prepared.

Where do you think the sow bugs will go? Will they seek out areas of darkness or light? Will they prefer dry, moist, or wet peat moss? Or will they roam randomly over the sand?

• Design some experiments of your own to find out whether sow bugs prefer cold, cool, or warm temperatures. Do they respond to touch? Do they possess a sense of smell? Can they see? Can they hear? Can they move backwards? Can they learn?

Earthworms and Light

Separate a large shoe box into three compartments by taping small pieces of cardboard across the box as shown in Figure 35. Leave about a 2-cm space between the bottom of the box and the bottom of the cardboard divider so that the worms can crawl from one compartment to another. Cut

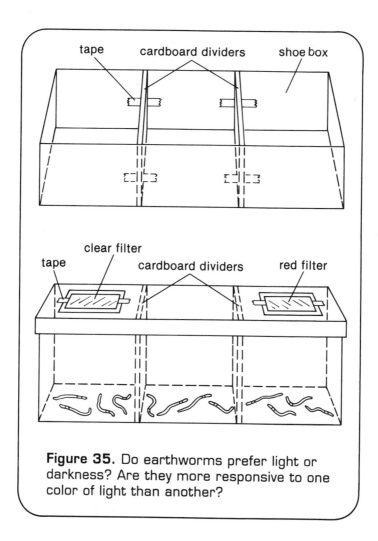

Figure 35. Do earthworms prefer light or darkness? Are they more responsive to one color of light than another?

openings about 7–8 cm on a side in the top of the box above each of the two end compartments. Tape clear plastic wrap over one opening and several layers of deep red cellophane or a transparent red plastic filter over the other. Cover the bottom of the box with moist paper towels and add a few earthworms to each compartment.

Leave the box under a bright light or near a window for about an hour. Where are the earthworms now? Are they still evenly distributed within the box? Do you have any evidence that earthworms can respond to light? Which—if either—light do they seem to avoid? Will they react in the same way if you use a green filter in place of the red? A blue filter in place of the red?

COLORED SHADOWS

MATERIALS NEEDED

- pencil
- clay
- white frosted light bulb and lamp
- red, blue, and green light bulbs
- 3 incandescent study lamps
- white wall or white paper screen

Unlike in the case of earthworms, you don't have to do an experiment to know that humans are sensitive to and respond to light. However, there are many things about our sense of sight that are fascinating and not thoroughly understood.

I happen to enjoy looking for colored shadows. They're quite common, but few people ever notice them. It never ceases to amaze me that a dark shadow turns yellow when illuminated by a combination of red and green light. Even though there are no wavelengths that we normally perceive as yellow, the combination of wavelengths falling on the shadow appears to us to be yellow. Somehow our brain sees a combination of red and green light as yellow.

If you look for them, you'll see colored shadows frequently. They're all around Christmas trees. They're evident when the red or blue lights of a fire truck or a police car fall on shadows cast by street or porch lights. Often they can be seen in the vicinity of sodium vapor lamps in parking lots or along streets.

In this experiment, you'll use red, blue, and green lights because all the colors we see can be made by mixing these three colored lights. Use a single unshaded frosted light bulb in a dark room to produce a shadow of a pencil supported by a small piece of clay as shown in Figure 36. The shadow should fall on a white wall or paper screen. The light should be on the side of the room farthest from the pencil. Red, blue, and green light bulbs in study lamps can be used to illuminate the shadow without casting a second shadow. As you can see, the shadow acquires a reddish color when illuminated by red light, a greenish color in green light, and a bluish color in blue light.

What is the color of the shadow when it is illuminated by both red and green light? By red and blue light? By blue and green light? By all three colored lights?

To understand why a shadow appears yellow when illuminated by red and green light, shine both red and green light (no white light) on a white screen. What color appears to be present where these two colors overlap? Similarly, red and blue lights mix to produce a color called magenta; blue and green lights produce a color called cyan when they are mixed.

Now cast *two* shadows of the pencil: one with the white light you used before and one with the

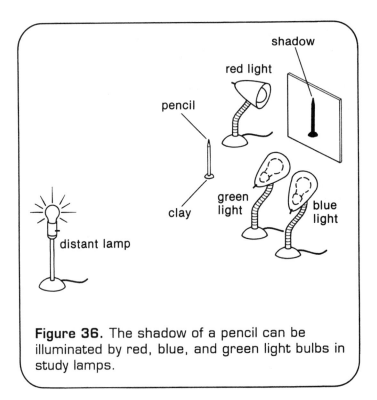

Figure 36. The shadow of a pencil can be illuminated by red, blue, and green light bulbs in study lamps.

red light. Place the red light so that the shadow it makes is close to the shadow cast by the more distant white light. The shadow cast by the white light appears red when illuminated by the red light. No surprise there! Now, look at the shadow cast by the red light that is illuminated by white light? Why do you think it is cyan in color?

Look at the colors of the two shadows cast by green and white light. By blue and white light. How do you explain the colors of these shadows?

•   What you saw when you viewed two shadows cast by white light and a primary colored light (red, green, or blue) may be related to *after-*

images—the images you see after you look at a bright light. To make a more systematic study of afterimages, place a bright-green square on a sheet of white paper. Stare at the square for about 30 seconds. Then remove the square and continue looking at the paper. What is the color of the square's afterimage? Repeat the experiment using squares made with the other two primary colors of light—red and blue. What are the colors of their afterimages?

Repeat the experiment again with the green square. While you are staring, notice the colored fringe that surrounds the green square. What is the color of the fringe? Can you predict the color of the fringe you'll see if you stare at a blue square? At a red square?

Do you think these afterimage effects are related to the colored shadows you saw cast by white light and a primary color of light? If so, how do you think they are related? Design and carry out experiments to test your hypothesis.

COLORED OBJECTS IN COLORED LIGHT

MATERIALS NEEDED

- red, blue, and green light bulbs
- white wall or white paper screen
- pieces of colored construction paper—red, blue, green, cyan, magenta, yellow, white, and black
- colored plastic filters or gels—red, blue, green, yellow, cyan, magenta

From the previous experiment, you know that shadows can be colored by the light that shines on them. If you've ever looked at cars in a parking lot illuminated by sodium vapor lamps, you know that cars appear to have a different color in yellow light than they do in ordinary white sunlight.

You can use the same colored light bulbs you used before to illuminate samples of colored construction paper. Can you predict what color a piece of green paper will appear to have in red light? In green light? In blue light? In a mixture of red and green light? In a mixture of blue and green light? In a mixture of red and blue light? Can you predict the color of blue paper or red paper in these different colored lights? How about yellow, cyan, magenta, black, and white paper in these different colored lights?

If you have pieces of colored plastic filters, such as the gels used on lights in theaters, you can look through the filter at light coming from the sky's horizon, **not the sun**, or from a bright white wall. It's not surprising that the light appears to be red when viewed through a red filter, blue when seen through a blue filter, or green when viewed through a green filter. But can you predict what color you'll see if the light passes through both a red and a blue filter before reaching your eye? A red and a green filter? How about a yellow and a red filter? A cyan and a blue filter? Other combinations?

• Cut your first initial from a piece of red paper and your last initial from a piece of blue paper. Do this twice. Paste one set of initials (red first initial and blue second initial) to a sheet of white paper. Paste the other set to a sheet of black paper. What do you expect to see if you look at each set of colored initials through a filter transparent to only red light? Try it! What do you see? How can you explain what you see? Can you now predict what you will see if you look at both sets of initials through a filter transparent to only blue light?

6

CHALLENGING EXPERIMENTS IN CHEMISTRY

The subject matter of chemistry, like that of biology, is very subtle. In physics, we can often feel the forces involved and see their effects, but the forces involved in chemical reactions are far too small to feel. They take place at the submicroscopic level of atoms and molecules. Nevertheless, many students find the study of chemistry appealing as well as challenging.

In this chapter, you'll find that the level of challenge increases as you move from one experiment to the next. The first experiment requires relatively little knowledge of chemistry and can be done in your own kitchen. The rest of the chemistry experiments will require some familiarity with chemistry or an understanding of energy and heat, which you can attain by doing some of the experiments in earlier chapters of this book. They will also require equipment that generally can be found only in science laboratories. Consequently, with the exception of the first experiment (Paper Towel Chemistry), **the experiments in this chapter should be performed in a science laboratory under the supervision of a** science teacher. You should also wear safety goggles and a laboratory apron while in the laboratory.

PAPER TOWEL CHEMISTRY

MATERIALS NEEDED

- different brands of paper towels: Bounty, VIVA, Scot-towels, Sparkle, Coronet, Brawny, etc.
- scissors or shears
- water
- graduated cylinder, 100 mL
- pencil
- ruler
- waxed paper
- board, book, or blocks
- clock or watch with second hand
- container for water
- tape and food coloring

The chemistry of paper towels is related to the principle of *capillarity*—the attraction between the molecules of a liquid and those of a solid that causes the liquid to "climb" up narrow glass tubes or the spaces between wood fibers. Since paper is made from wood, capillarity in paper towels is the result of the narrow spaces between closely packed wood fibers and the way the towels are manufactured. You've probably seen advertisements about the "quicker-picker-upper." Most science students enjoy testing the claims made in advertisements, and that's just what you'll do in these experiments. You'll measure the amount of water absorbed by equal areas of different brands of paper towels as well as the rate at

Which of the many brands of paper towel picks
up the most water per weight per paper towel?

which the water is absorbed. To do this you'll need to gather a number of different brands of paper towels that you can find at a supermarket, such as Bounty, which claims to be the quicker-picker-upper; VIVA; Scottowels; Sparkle; Coronet; and Brawny. Be sure to record the price of each roll of paper towel you buy as well as the total area and mass of the towels. What is the price of each brand in terms of cents per unit area? In cents per unit mass? What is the mass density of each brand in grams per unit area?

In order to test equal areas, take one sheet from each roll. Cut all the towels so that they have the same area as the brand with the smallest area. Then test each brand, in turn, by slowly immersing a folded towel into a tall graduated cylinder filled with water. Remove the towel and let any excess water drip back into the cylinder. Repeat the experiment with each towel several times to be sure your results are consistent. Record the average volume of water absorbed by each towel. Since the density of water is 1 g/cm^3, the volume of water absorbed, in cubic centimeters (cm^3) or milliliters (mL), is numerically equal to the mass of water absorbed in grams. What is the mass of water absorbed per unit area and per unit mass of towel for each brand?

Which brand of towel absorbs most water per unit area? Per unit mass of towel? Per penny spent?

To compare the rate at which different towels absorb water, cut strips of equal area, say 4 cm × 25 cm, from each brand of towel. Make pencil marks across the strips at 1-cm intervals starting from a zero about 3 or 4 cm from the end that is to be placed in a container of water as shown in Figure 37. Water will be absorbed into the towel and move horizontally along the strip of towel that rests on a flat piece of waxed paper supported by a board, book, or blocks. (Wax will resist wetting by the water, which will, therefore, remain in the towel.) For each towel, record the elapsed time for the water to pass each 1-cm marking. Since you've already measured the mass of water per area in the towel, you can calculate the mass of water that has been absorbed after any given time.

Which towel is the quicker-picker-upper? Is the rate that water flows into the towel constant? If not, does the rate increase or decrease with time?

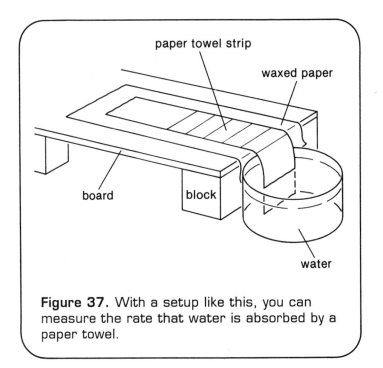

Figure 37. With a setup like this, you can measure the rate that water is absorbed by a paper towel.

Does the towel with the fastest absorbing rate have smaller spaces between the fibers? This would cause it to have greater capillary action than the other towels, which would mean that water would rise to a greater vertical height in this towel than in others. To check up on this idea, cut 1-in-wide strips of the maximum possible length from each of the brands of paper towels you tested. Use tape to suspend them *vertically* and side by side from a stick, kitchen chair or stool, or kitchen cabinet above a countertop. The lower end of each towel should touch a container of colored water (use a few drops of food coloring) as does the end of the towel shown in Figure 37. In which towel does the water rise to the highest level? What can you conclude?

In this last experiment all the towels had the same width. What would happen if you varied the width of the towel and therefore the surface area? Do you think the water would rise to the same height in towel strips with different widths? Try it! Were you right?

How can you explain the results? Don't forget that water can also evaporate from the towel. What effect would evaporation have on the height to which the water rises? How could you eliminate or greatly reduce the evaporation of water from the towel?

• The thickness of a paper towel is difficult to determine because it varies so much; however, the thickness of a sheet of aluminum foil is quite uniform. Given a ruler, a balance sensitive to at least 0.1 g, and the fact that aluminum has a density of 2.7 g/cm^3, determine the thickness of a sheet of aluminum foil.

THE ATOMIC MASS OF MAGNESIUM

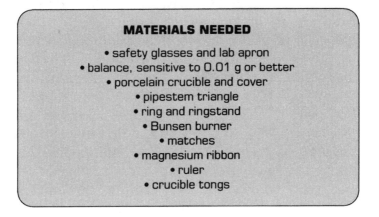

MATERIALS NEEDED

- safety glasses and lab apron
- balance, sensitive to 0.01 g or better
- porcelain crucible and cover
- pipestem triangle
- ring and ringstand
- Bunsen burner
- matches
- magnesium ribbon
- ruler
- crucible tongs

By the early nineteenth century chemists knew that oxygen was an element that combined with many other substances to form compounds called oxides. Some reactions were rapid, as when something burned; other reactions, such as the rusting of iron, were very slow.

These chemists also knew that hydrogen was an element and that its atoms were probably the lightest to be found. Consequently, they assigned hydrogen atoms a mass of 1 atomic mass unit (amu). Today we know that the mass of a hydrogen atom is 1.67×10^{-24} g, but they had no way of knowing the actual mass.

There was evidence that water molecules were formed by the union of two hydrogen atoms with one oxygen atom, which was represented by the formula H_2O. However, Thomas Dalton, who formulated the atomic theory, maintained that water molecules were a 1:1 union of oxygen and hydrogen atoms and that the correct formula was HO, not H_2O. Since they knew the mass ratio of hydrogen to oxygen in water was 1:8, they played it safe and assigned oxygen a mass of 16 amu. In that way, hydrogen would never have to be assigned a mass less than 1 amu.

By causing oxygen to react with known masses of other elements, chemists determined the atomic masses of these elements. In this experiment you'll see how they did it by determining the mass of oxygen that combines with a known mass of magnesium. Rather than use pure oxygen, we'll take advantage of the fact that air is 21 percent oxygen. Of the remaining 79 percent, all but 1 percent of it is nitrogen, which does not react appreciably with magnesium, and practically all the rest is argon, an inert gas that is virtually nonreactive.

After putting on your **safety glasses and lab apron**, begin the experiment as shown in Figure 38 by using a Bunsen burner to heat a porcelain crucible and cover supported by a pipestem triangle. This will remove any moisture that might be on the porcelain. When they have cooled, weigh the crucible and cover to at least the nearest 0.01 g. Wind a piece of magnesium ribbon about 20 cm long into a cone shape that will fit into the crucible. Add the cover to the crucible and reweigh. What is the mass of the magnesium in the crucible?

Now heat the crucible and its covered contents with the Bunsen burner. After about 20 minutes, use crucible tongs to lift one side of the cover a little so that air may enter. **Do not remove the cover** because if you do, some of the white, smokelike magnesium oxide (MgO) may escape. Continue heating for another 5 minutes, lifting

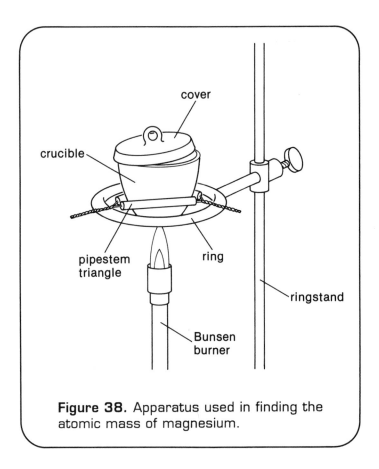

Figure 38. Apparatus used in finding the atomic mass of magnesium.

the cover slightly every 30 seconds to allow more air to enter.

Now, slide the cover back a bit to form a crescent-shaped opening that will allow air to enter the crucible. Continue heating for another 20 minutes. When the crucible, contents, and cover have cooled, reweigh them.

Heat for another 5 minutes, cool, and reweigh. Continue to do this until there is no further change in mass. How much oxygen combined with the magnesium?

Assuming that atoms of oxygen and magnesium combine in a 1:1 ratio, what is the atomic mass of magnesium? (Remember, the atomic mass of oxygen is defined as 16 units.)

HESS'S LAW

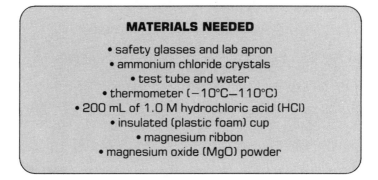

MATERIALS NEEDED

- safety glasses and lab apron
- ammonium chloride crystals
- test tube and water
- thermometer (−10°C−110°C)
- 200 mL of 1.0 M hydrochloric acid (HCl)
- insulated (plastic foam) cup
- magnesium ribbon
- magnesium oxide (MgO) powder

In Chapter 3 you learned how to measure the transfer of heat. Many chemical reactions are accompanied by the release or absorption of thermal energy. The burning of hydrogen or carbon in the presence of oxygen is an example of a reaction where heat is released. After putting on your **safety glasses and lab apron**, add a small amount of ammonium chloride crystals to about a third of a test tube of water. What happens to the temperature of the solution when ammonium chloride dissolves in water?

We may express the heat added to, or released from, a chemical reaction by including it in the equation for the reaction. For example, when a mole of hydrogen burns, 57.8 kcal are released. To show that in equation form, we can write:

$$H_2(g) + \frac{1}{2} O_2(g) \rightarrow H_2O(g) + 57.8 \, kcal.$$

The symbol (g) means that the substance is in the gaseous state; (s) stands for the solid state, and (l) for the liquid state. The state must be specified because, as you know from Chapter 3, energy is released or absorbed during a change of state. If the reaction proceeds in such a way that the product is *liquid* water at 25°C, the equation is written

$$H_2(g) + \frac{1}{2}O_2(g) \rightarrow H_2O(l) + 68.3 \text{ kcal.}$$

From the law of conservation of energy, the equation for the decomposition of water into its elements, which is usually done by electrolysis, would be written as the reverse of the previous equation,

$$H_2O(l) + 68.3 \text{ kcal} \rightarrow H_2(g) + \frac{1}{2}O_2(g)$$

According to *Hess's law*, when a reaction can be expressed as the algebraic sum of a sequence of two or more other reactions, the heat of reaction is the algebraic sum of the heats of these reactions. For example, suppose we want to know how much energy is released when carbon burns to form carbon dioxide. Suppose we know the heats of reaction for the first three of the following equations. We can use those equations to find the heat produced per mole of carbon burned by rewriting them as shown in the second three equations, and then adding them to find the equation and heat value we seek.

$$CO(g) + H_2(g) \rightarrow H_2O(g) + C(s) + 31.4 \text{ kcal}$$
$$CO(g) + \frac{1}{2}O_2(g) \rightarrow CO_2(g) + 67.6 \text{ kcal}$$
$$H_2O(g) + 57.8 \text{ kcal} \rightarrow H_2(g) + \frac{1}{2}O_2(g)$$

$$H_2O(g) + C(s) + 31.4 \text{ kcal} \rightarrow CO(g) + H_2(g)$$

$$CO(g) + \frac{1}{2} O_2(g) \rightarrow CO_2(g) + 67.6 \text{ kcal}$$

$$H_2(g) + \frac{1}{2} O_2(g) \rightarrow H_2O(g) + 57.8 \text{ kcal}$$

$$\overline{\quad C(s) + O_2(g) \rightarrow CO_2(g) + 94.0 \text{ kcal} \quad}$$

When magnesium burns to form magnesium oxide (MgO), a considerable amount of heat per mole is transferred from the system to the surroundings. It is difficult to measure this heat directly, but by applying Hess's law to a number of other, less violent reactions, or reactions where the heat changes per mole are known, the heat released per mole of magnesium burned can be determined.

Consider the following reactions:

$$H_2(g) + \frac{1}{2} O_2(g) \rightarrow H_2O(1) + 68.3 \text{ kcal}$$

$$Mg(s) + 2 HCl(1) \rightarrow MgCl_2(s) + H_2(g)$$
$$\overline{MgCl(s) + H_2O(1) \rightarrow MgO(s) + 2 HCl(1)}$$

What is the algebraic sum of these reactions? To find the additional information you need, you will have to carry out the following chemical reactions. **Be sure to wear safety glasses and a lab apron** as you do these experiments. Should you accidentally spill any acid, rinse it away with lots of cold water.

• Use a thermometer to determine the temperature of 100 mL of 1.0 M hydrochloric acid (HCl) in an insulated cup. You'll introduce an error no greater than 10 percent if you consider the specific heat of the solution to be 1.0 cal/g/°C. Now, add 0.01 mole of magnesium ribbon to the acid. What gas do you think is produced when these two substances react? What is the temperature after the reaction has gone to completion? How much heat would be released or absorbed per mole of magnesium?

• Again, determine the temperature of 100 mL of 1.0 M HCl in an insulated cup. Then add 0.01 mole of magnesium oxide (MgO) powder to the acid. Stir until all the solid has reacted and note the temperature change. How much heat is released or absorbed per mole of MgO reacted?

From the data supplied and from the results of your experiments, determine the heat released when 1 mole of Mg burns.

THE SOLUBILITY PRODUCT OF LEAD IODIDE (PbI$_2$)

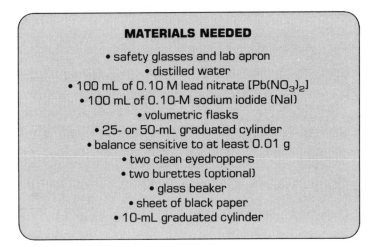

MATERIALS NEEDED

• safety glasses and lab apron
• distilled water
• 100 mL of 0.10 M lead nitrate [Pb(NO$_3$)$_2$]
• 100 mL of 0.10-M sodium iodide (NaI)
• volumetric flasks
• 25- or 50-mL graduated cylinder
• balance sensitive to at least 0.01 g
• two clean eyedroppers
• two burettes (optional)
• glass beaker
• sheet of black paper
• 10-mL graduated cylinder

Many chemical reactions reach a state of equilibrium in which the rate that the reactants are combining to form products is equal to the rate that the products are combining to form the reactants. Nothing appears to be happening, but by using radioactive substances it can be shown that both reactions are taking place. The equilibrium exists because the two rates of reaction are equal. For example, in the reaction $A + B \rightarrow C + D$, as the concentration of C and D increases, the rate of the reverse reaction $C + D \rightarrow A + B$ increases. Finally, the two rates become equal and the system reaches equilibrium. The equilibrium reaction can be expressed as

$$A + B \leftrightarrow C + D.$$

Experiments show that when a reaction like the one above reaches equilibrium, the product of the concentration of the products divided by the product of the concentration of the reactants will be a constant, K, characteristic of that particular reaction for a given temperature. That is,

$$\frac{[C] \times [D]}{[A] \times [B]} = K.$$

The symbols [and] which enclose the symbols for the chemicals stand for "concentration of"; thus, $[CO_2]$ means "concentration of carbon dioxide." The concentration is usually expressed in moles per liter.

For a more complicated reaction at equilibrium, such as

$$mA + nB \leftrightarrow xC + yD,$$

where m, n, x, and y are coefficients, the equilibrium expression is given by

$$\frac{[C]^x \times [D]^y}{[A]^m \times [B]^n} = K.$$

For two ions, such as the silver (Ag^+) and the chloride (Cl^-) ions, that combine to form a relatively insoluble salt, the equation that expresses the equilibrium is

$$AgCl_{(s)} \leftrightarrow Ag^+ \text{ (aq)} + Cl^- \text{ (aq)},$$

where (s) indicates that the salt is in the solid state and (aq) indicates that the ion is dissolved in water (an aqueous solution). Since the concentration of a solid can't change (its density is fixed), the equilibrium expression for this equilibrium is usually written without the concentration of the solid. Because the concentration of the solid can't change, it can have no effect on the concentration of the ions.

Therefore, the expression for such an equilibrium is written

$$K_{sp} = [Ag^+][Cl^-].$$

The equilibrium constant, K_{sp}, is called the solubility product constant. Whenever the product of the concentration of the ions exceeds the K_{sp}, a precipitate will form.

If the ions combine in some ratio other than 1:1, the expression is based on the equilibrium reaction, $mA + nB \leftrightarrow xC + yD$, described previously. For example, when tricalcium phosphate [$Ca_3(PO_4)_2$], which is only slightly soluble, dissolves in water, the equilibrium equation is

$$Ca_3(PO_4)_{2(s)} \leftrightarrow 3\ Ca^{+2}_{(aq)} + 2\ PO_4^{-3}_{(aq)}.$$

The K_{sp} for this salt is given by

$$K_{sp} = [Ca^{+2}]^3[PO_4^{-3}]^2.$$

The solubility of tricalcium phosphate is found to be 3.92×10^{-16} moles per liter. As you can see from the equation, for each mole of the salt that dissolves, the solution will contain 3 moles of calcium ions (Ca^{+3}) and 2 moles of phosphate ions $[PO_4)^{-3}]$. Thus, the Ksp for this salt is given by

$$Ksp = (3 \times 3.92 \times 10^{-6})^3(2 \times 3.92 \times 10^{-6})^2 = 1.00 \times 10^{-25}.$$

The equation that expresses the equilibrium between solid lead iodide and its ions in solution is

$$PbI_{2(s)} \leftrightarrow Pb^{+2}_{(sq)} + 2\,I^-_{(sq)}.$$

To find the Ksp for lead iodide (PbI_2), you will need to know the concentration of lead ions and iodide ions at the point where equilibrium is reached. To find this point, **put on your safety glasses and lab apron** before you prepare 100 mL of 0.10 M lead nitrate $[Pb(NO_3)_2]$ and 100 mL of 0.10 M sodium iodide (NaI). Prepare these solutions very carefully, using volumetric flasks, distilled water, and a balance sensitive to at least 0.01 g.

Next, carefully calibrate an eyedropper so that you know how many drops it delivers per milliliter (mL) and, therefore, the volume of 1 drop. (If you prefer, you can place both solutions in burettes.)

Measure out exactly 25.0 mL of 0.10 M lead nitrate and pour it into a clean 100-mL glass beaker. Place the beaker on a sheet of black paper. Fill a 10-mL graduated cylinder with 0.10-M sodium iodide and add this solution drop by drop to the lead nitrate solution as you constantly stir the mixture. When the product of the concentration of lead ion and iodide ion reaches the value of the Ksp, lead iodide will begin to precipitate. When you reach this point of saturation, a faint yellow color will appear (lead iodide is a yellow solid) and will persist even after stirring. The black paper beneath the beaker provides a background that makes the faint precipitate of lead iodide easier to see and will prevent you from going beyond the end point.

How many drops of sodium iodide did you add to the lead nitrate to reach the end point? How many milliliters did you add? What was the total volume of liquid in the beaker when you reached the end point? How many moles of lead ion (Pb^{+2}) and iodide ion (I^-) were present when the precipitate was first noted? What was the concentration of these ions at the end point? What is the Ksp of lead iodide according to your results?

Repeat the process using a clean eyedropper, but this time add *lead nitrate* solution drop by drop to 25 mL of sodium iodide solution. What happens after the addition of a single drop? Can you figure out why?

To prevent this problem, dilute both solutions to 0.01 M before again adding drops of the lead nitrate to 25 mL of the sodium iodide.

How many milliliters of lead nitrate did you add before reaching an end point? How many moles of each ion were in the beaker at the saturation point? What was the concentration of each ion at the end point? What is the Ksp for lead iodide according to these results? Does it agree with the previous value? If the two values don't agree, can you explain why?

THE RATE OF A CHEMICAL REACTION

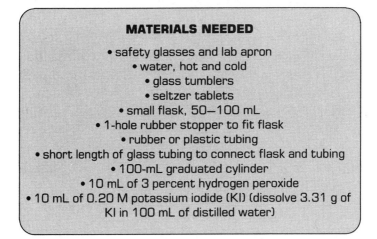

MATERIALS NEEDED

- safety glasses and lab apron
- water, hot and cold
- glass tumblers
- seltzer tablets
- small flask, 50–100 mL
- 1-hole rubber stopper to fit flask
- rubber or plastic tubing
- short length of glass tubing to connect flask and tubing
- 100-mL graduated cylinder
- 10 mL of 3 percent hydrogen peroxide
- 10 mL of 0.20 M potassium iodide (KI) (dissolve 3.31 g of KI in 100 mL of distilled water)

Most people know that the rate at which a chemical reaction proceeds depends on the temperature. It's easy to show that this is true: simply add one seltzer tablet to a glass of cold water and a second to a glass of hot water. You'll see that the fizzing is much faster in the warmer water.

It's also true that the rate of a reaction is often related to the concentration of the reactants. If you drop two seltzer tablets into a glass of water, the reaction is more rapid; that is, it takes less than twice the time for a single tablet to react.

In this experiment, you'll try to determine how the rate at which hydrogen peroxide (H_2O_2) decomposes is related to its concentration and to the concentration of a catalyst. The reaction is summarized by the chemical equation

$$2\,H_2O_2 \rightarrow 2H_2O + O_2 \text{ (gas)}$$

Some reactions, such as the rusting of
iron (inset), proceed very slowly. Others, such as
the burning of a fuel, take place rapidly.

This reaction is a good one to investigate because it goes very nearly to completion, the rate is easy to measure because the reaction proceeds relatively slowly, and one of the products (oxygen) has minimal solubility in water and its volume can be measured quite accurately.

The reaction is too slow to determine in any practical way, but a catalyst, potassium iodide (KI), increases the reaction rate to a point where it can be measured.

After putting on your **safety glasses and lab apron**, examine Figure 39. It shows the apparatus used in the experiment. The water bath allows you to keep the temperature constant. Why should the temperature be kept constant?

The reaction takes place in a small flask. The pressure of the oxygen produced forces the gas through the rubber or plastic tubing into an inverted 100-mL graduated cylinder that is filled with water. The bubbles of oxygen rise to the top of the cylinder, where the volume of the gas can be measured periodically.

Measure out 10 mL of 3 percent H_2O_2 in a small graduated cylinder. Since the density of such a solution is very nearly that of water, you may assume that you have 0.30 g of H_2O_2 (0.03 × 10 g). Since a molecule of H_2O_2 has 34 atomic mass units ([2 × 1] + [2 × 16]), a mole of this substance weighs 34 g. In the 10 mL of solution there is 0.0088 mole of H_2O_2 ([0.30 g]/[34 g per mole]). The molar concentration (M) of H_2O_2, expressed in moles per liter, is, therefore,

$$\frac{0.0088 \text{ mole}}{0.01 \text{ L}} = 0.88 \text{ mole/L} \quad \text{or} \quad 0.88 \text{ M}.$$

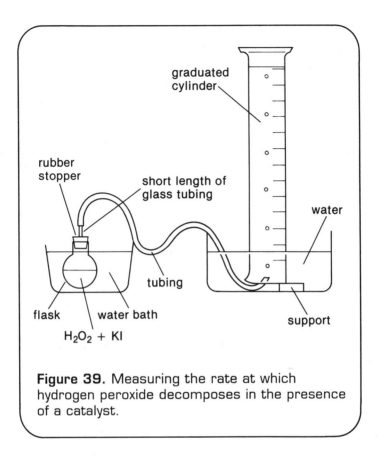

Figure 39. Measuring the rate at which hydrogen peroxide decomposes in the presence of a catalyst.

After you add 10 mL of 0.20 M KI, the concentration of the solution of H_2O_2 will become 0.44 M. What will be the concentration of the KI?

Now pour the 10 mL of KI into the flask and swirl thoroughly to mix the two solutions. Insert the stopper into the neck of the flask and continue to swirl. Be sure to keep the flask in the water bath so that the temperature within the flask remains constant. Have a partner hold the end of the tubing connected to the rubber stopper under the water near the inverted graduated cylinder. When bubbles of gas begin to emerge from the tubing, stick the end of the tube under the cylinder and start the stopwatch or note the position of the sweep second hand or mode of a clock or watch.

Continue to swirl the flask in a rapid and consistent manner as your partner records the time needed to collect 5 mL, 10 mL, 15 mL, . . . , 80 mL of oxygen. Once you've collected all the data, you're ready to begin your analysis.

Since 2 moles of H_2O_2 are required to produce 1 mole of O_2, you can use the number of moles of oxygen collected to determine the concentration of peroxide remaining in the flask. For example, let's assume that the temperature is 20°C (293 K) and the barometer is at 750 mm of mercury ($9.96 \times 10^{-4} N/m^2$) when you have collected 10 mL of oxygen. Under these conditions of temperature and pressure, a mole of gas, which occupies 22.4 L at 0°C (273 K) and atmospheric pressure (760 mm of mercury, or 1.01×10^5 Pa), will have a volume of

$$22.4 \text{ L} \times \frac{760}{750} \times \frac{293}{273} = 24.4 \text{ L.}$$

Hence, the number of moles of oxygen in 10 mL of the gas is

$$\frac{10}{2.44 \times 10^4} = 4.1 \times 10^{-4} \text{ mole.}$$

Since 4.1×10^{-4} mole of oxygen has been produced, 8.2×10^{-4} mole of H_2O_2 has decomposed. Thus,

$(8.8 \times 10^{-3}) - (8.2 \times 10^{-4}) = 8.0 \times 10^{-3}$ mole of peroxide.

The concentration of the remaining 8.0×10^{-3} mole of peroxide is

$$\frac{8.0 \times 10^{-3} \text{ mole}}{1.0 \times 10^{-2} \text{ L}} = 0.80 \text{ M}.$$

You can use this approach to calculate the remaining concentration of H_2O_2 for every volume of oxygen measured. From your data and calculations, plot a graph of the number of moles of H_2O_2 remaining as a function of time. Since the volume in the flask is constant, the concentration of H_2O_2 is directly proportional to the number of moles of H_2O_2 that remain.

Suppose your graph looks like the one in Figure 40. By taking the slope of the graph at any point in time as shown, you can determine the rate of the reaction.

$$\text{Reaction rate} = \frac{\Delta C}{\Delta t},$$

where ΔC is the change in concentration of H_2O_2 and Δt is the change in time.

Once you have obtained values for the slope of the graph for as wide a range as possible, plot another graph. This time plot the reaction rate in moles per minute as a function of the concentration of H_2O_2, that is, the number of moles of H_2O_2 remaining in the solution.

How is the rate of the reaction related to the concentration of H_2O_2?

- Design and carry out an experiment to see whether the concentration of the catalyst (KI) has any effect on the rate of the reaction.

• If you have studied chemical reaction rates and rate laws, use your results to develop a hypothetical reaction mechanism for this reaction that is in agreement with the rate you have measured.

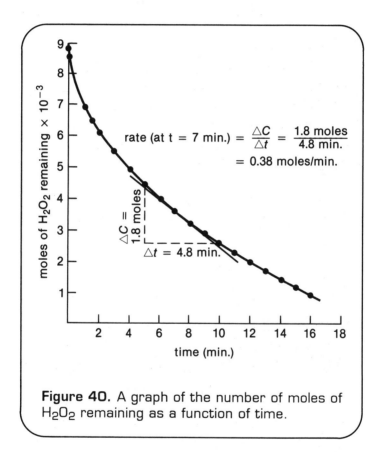

Figure 40. A graph of the number of moles of H_2O_2 remaining as a function of time.

APPENDIX: SCIENCE SUPPLY COMPANIES

Carolina Biological
Supply Co.
2700 York Road
Burlington, NC 27215

Central Scientific Co.
(CENCO)
11222 Melrose Avenue
Franklin Park, IL 60131

Connecticut Valley Biological Supply Co., Inc.
82 Valley Road
Southampton, MA 01073

Delta Education
P.O. Box M
Nashua, NH 03061

Edmund Scientific Co.
101 East Gloucester Pike
Barrington, NJ 08007

Fisher Scientific Co.
4901 W. LeMoyne Street
Chicago, IL 60651

Frey Scientific Co.
905 Hickory Lane
Mansfield, OH 44905

McKilligan Supply Corp.
435 Main Street
Johnson City, NY 13790

Nasco Science
901 Janesville Road
Fort Atkinson, WI 53538

Nasco West Inc.
P.O. Box 3837
Modesto, CA 95352

Prentice Hall
Allyn & Bacon
Equipment Division
10 Oriskany Drive
Tonawanda, NY
14150-6781

Schoolmasters Science
P.O. Box 1941
Ann Arbor, MI 48106

Science Kit & Boreal
Laboratories
777 East Park Drive
Tonawanda, NY
14150-6782
or
P.O. Box 2726
Santa Fe Springs, CA
90670-4490

Wards Natural Science
Establishment, Inc.
5100 West Henrietta Road
P.O. Box 92912
Rochester, NY 14692

FOR FURTHER READING

Gardner Robert. *Energy Projects for Young Scientists*, New York: Franklin Watts, 1987.

———. *Experimenting with Illusions*, New York: Franklin Watts, 1990.

———. *Experimenting with Inventions*, New York: Franklin Watts, 1990.

———. *Experimenting with Light*, New York: Franklin Watts, 1991.

———. *Experimenting with Sound*, New York: Franklin Watts, 1991.

———. *Famous Experiments You Can Do*, New York: Franklin Watts, 1990.

———. *Ideas for Science Projects*, New York: Franklin Watts, 1986.

———. *Magic Through Science*, New York: Doubleday, 1978.

———. *More Ideas for Science Projects*, New York: Franklin Watts, 1989.

———. *Projects in Space Science*, New York: Messner, 1988.

Gardner, Robert, and David Webster. *Moving Right Along*. New York: Doubleday, 1978.

Haber-Schaim et al. *PSSC Physics*. Dubuque, Iowa: Kendall/Hunt, 1991.

Webster, David. *Spider Watching*. New York: Messner, 1984.

INDEX

ABOUT THE AUTHOR

Robert Gardner taught physical science, physics, chemistry, and biology for more than thirty years at Salisbury School in Salisbury, Connecticut, prior to his retirement. A *School Library Journal* reviewer has called him "the master of the science experiment book," and his books have won numerous awards and citations. Robert Gardner's other books include *Ideas for Science Projects, More Ideas for Science Projects, Famous Experiments You Can Do, Experimenting with Light,* and *Experimenting with Sound.* Also available from Franklin Watts is *Robert Gardner's Favorite Science Experiments,* which complements the book you hold in your hands. Mr. Gardner lives in North Eastham, Massachusetts, on Cape Cod, with his wife, Natalie.